Scott Collins' Fretboard Visualization Series

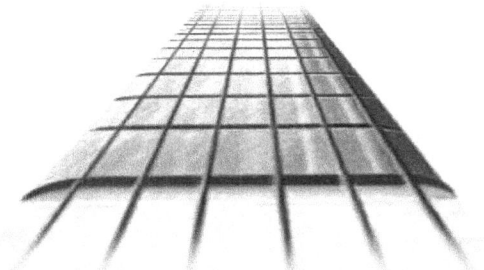

The Minor Pentatonic Scale

This book has been created with the best of intentions and a DIY aesthetic. With that in mind, a large font size has been used here to facilitate reading as it is assumed that the reader will have this book on a music stand.

It may offend your aesthetic sensibilities but your eye's will thank you later.

2013 Edition
ISBN: 978-1-300-49974-9
Copyright © Scott Collins 2013

2

For more information, please contact:

guitar.blueprint@gmail.com

or visit

http://www.guitarchitecture.org

Thanks and Acknowledgements

Special thanks are due to the following people who went above and beyond any reasonable requests for assistance:

- John Harper and Chris Fitzpatrick of FnH Guitars have been better friends than I could ask for and also happen to make the best instruments I've had the pleasure of playing!

- Spouses of writers tend to have a unique stress placed on them. This is especially true when they happen to be better writers than you and get roped into edits and re-writes. My love, gratitude and thanks to the long put-upon Candace Burnham.

Thanks to everyone who bought Fiverr editions of this as an e-book and pre-release editions of the *GuitArchitect's Guide To*: books. Your support has been affirming, humbling and greatly appreciated!

Additional thanks need to go to those who helped in one way or another even when it pained them to do so:

Susan Allen, Carl Barc, Patty Barkas, Reg Bloor, Craig Bunch, Daren Burns, Phil Clevenger, Scott Crosby, Caroline Dillon, Jose Duque, Carmina Escobar, Jon Finn, Stuart Fox, Geoff Chase, Vinny Golia, Joe Gore, Lulu Hoeller, Leslie Johnson, Doug Kearns, Will Kennedy, Rohin Khemani, Eric Klerks, Ulrich Krieger, Andre LaFosse, Chris Lavender, Betty Lee, Don McLeod, Gary Mairs, Mike Mallory, Tim Monaghan, Chad Perry, Moby Pomerance, Jonathan Reid, Jack Sanders, Miroslav Tadic, Ergin "Tex" Ozler, Joe Rauen, Mike Reagan, Jack Sanders, Pawel Sek, Teresa Sienkiewicz, Koven Smith, Fernando Vigueras, Jen Ward, Jonathan Wilson.

And last, but not least, thank you dear reader.

Table Of Contents

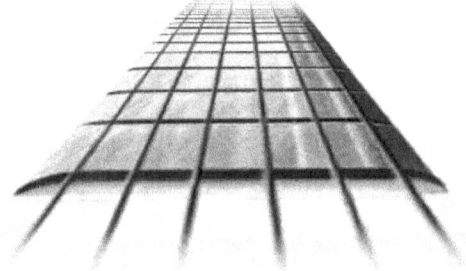

Table Of Contents

5

Table Of Contents

6

Table Of Contents

7

GuitArchitecture And The Minor Pentatonic Scale

GuitArchitecture is a term I use to describe my visual approach to playing guitar. A key component of GuitArchitecture is a modular approach called *Sonic Visualization* that associates sounds with fretboard patterns for the purpose of realizing and modifiyng those sounds in real-time.

Along these lines, this book shows how to break minor pentatonic shapes into modular patterns that can fit like puzzle pieces across a guitar fingerboard. I've used E Minor Pentatonic (E, G, B, A and D) for the majority of the instruction here.   A few clarifying notes follow:

1. Since E Minor Pentatonic and G Major Pentatonic are the same scale, all of the fingering patterns here are applicable to the relative major pentatonic as well.

2. While this book focuses exclusively on the minor pentatonic scale, the methodology can also be adapted to the six-note E Blues scale (E, G, A, A♯/B♭, B and D) or any other scale or mode.

The book has been broken up into a series of short chapters that ultimately demonstrate other ways to break out of the pentatonic box shape (including one-string patterns and pentatonic chords).

I hope it helps you with your playing goals!

Theoretical and Technical Considerations

This text reviews some musical concepts, but the reader should have a basic understanding of intervals, chords, major/minor key sets and the ability to read standard notation (or tablature) or review these concepts, if necessary.

While a separate instructional material focusing specifically on practicing and technique is in development, a full exploration of music fundamentals is outside of the scope of this book. If the reader has specific technical questions regarding picking, hammer-ons, pull offs, and/or tapping, they should seek out a qualified teacher before fully embarking on this process.

If one's basic technique is flawed as a starting point, no amount of repetition will overcome those deficiencies.

In any practice or performance situation, try to focus on **tone** and (hand) **tension**. As you're playing, ask yourself the following questions:

- Can you hear every note clearly?
- Are they equal in volume and tone?
- How does it feel to play them?
- Are your hands relaxed (picking and fretting)?
- If you practice with too much tension, you will play with too much tension, and it will undermine your ability to execute.
- If you feel pain in your hands or forearms stop playing immediately!

Finally, while rhythmic variation is encouraged, playing in time (i.e. with a time keeping device like a metronome, recording or a drum sequence) is absolutely essential to optimizing performance.

Section I:

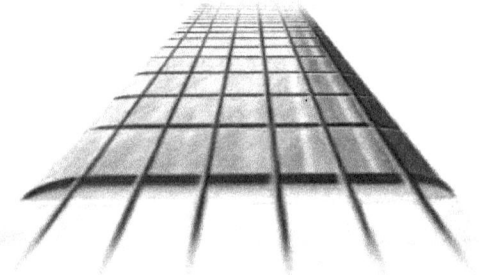

Two-String Patterns

Understanding "The Box" Pentatonic Shape

In lesson material, minor pentatonic scales are often presented with a fingerboard pattern that looks like this:

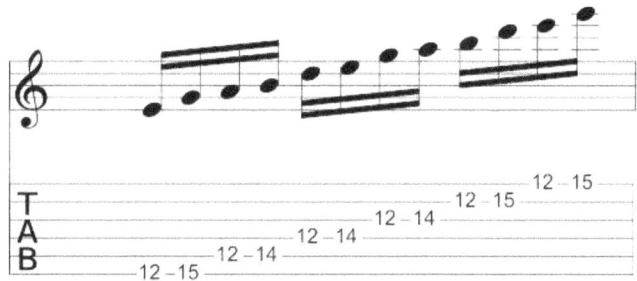

This positional "box" pattern works fine for a number of things but to get into lower and higher notes, you're going to have to break out of that shape.

11

The way I was taught to do this involved learning every inversion of this scale (i.e. being able to play the scale in any position and starting from any note of the scale) but I found this approach confusing and difficult to adapt to other keys.

I had a major conceptual breakthrough when I realized that my difficulty in linking things together came from trying to see the guitar as a series of six-string shapes. In examining the fretboard shapes closer I realized that:

The guitar is three sets of strings, tuned in 4ths.

This might not sound like a radical assertion, but it certainly is in its performance implications.

Looking at a guitar as three sets of strings with a uniform tuning means that any shape on one of those string sets will produce the same sound on the next string set.

In other words, the guitar is a set of modular two-string shapes that all interlock together.

Visualizing this will save a great deal of time when learning how the shapes fit together on the fingerboard.

The first step is to see how the scale sits on a set of two strings and then adapt it to positional playing. To start this process, I'll demonstrate playing E Minor Pentatonic using only the E and B strings.

Note:

I *strongly* recommend that the following examples should be practiced with a metronome, with strict alternate picking (or i-m for fingerstyle players), and (initially) played over either an E minor chord or a bass note E to hear the harmonic context for the scale.

Two-String E Minor Pentatonic Patterns

Pattern 1: (Starts from the root: E)

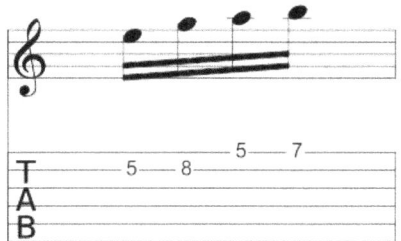

Pattern 2: (Starts from the ♭3rd: G)

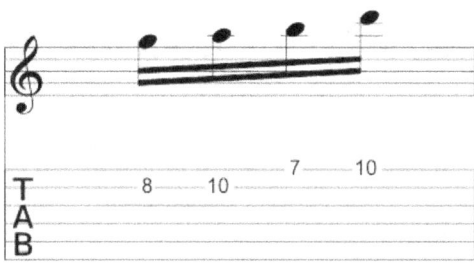

Pattern 3: (Starts from the 4th: A)

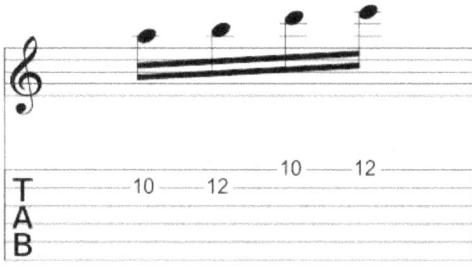

Pattern 4: (Starts from the 5th: B)

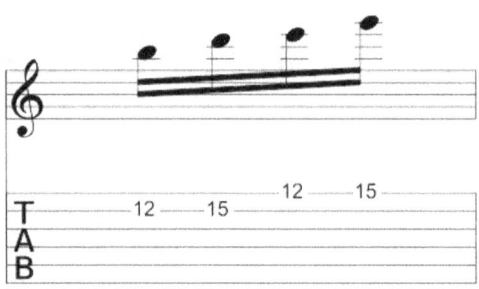

14

Pattern 5: (Starts from the ♭7th: D)

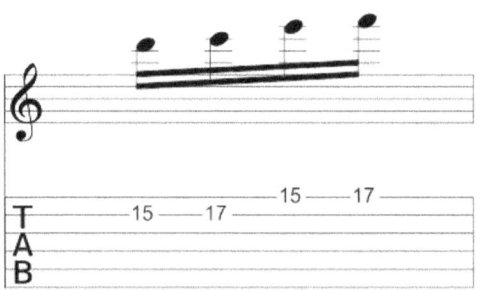

Once you're familiar with these initial patterns, the next step is to examine how these can interlock as a sequenced pattern on the same two strings.

Vertical (Two-String) Ascending Patterns

On two strings, the patterns link together in numeric order (i.e. 1, 2, 3, 4, 5).

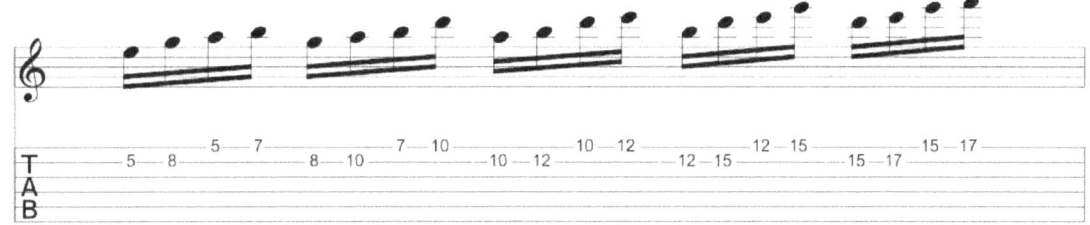

Pattern 1   Pattern 2   Pattern 3   Pattern 4   Pattern 5

Continuing this sequence, after Pattern 5 comes Pattern 1:

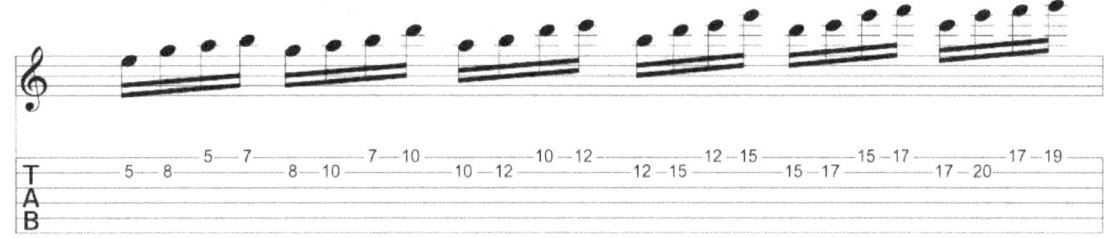

Pattern 1   Pattern 2   Pattern 3   Pattern 4   Pattern 5   Pattern 1

This also works in reverse. Below Pattern 1 is Pattern 5.

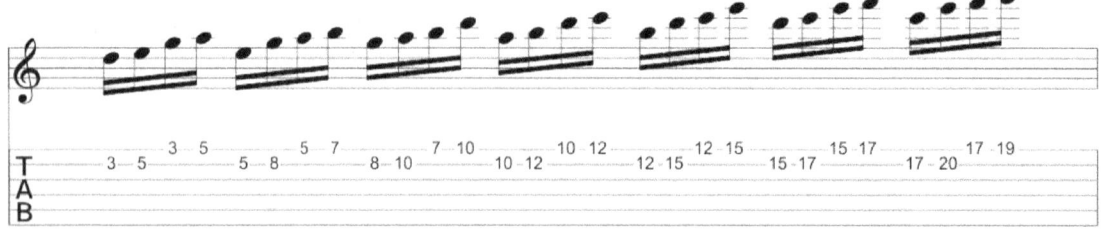

Pattern 5   Pattern 1   etc.

Pattern 4 starts the entire cycle using open notes on the B and E strings.

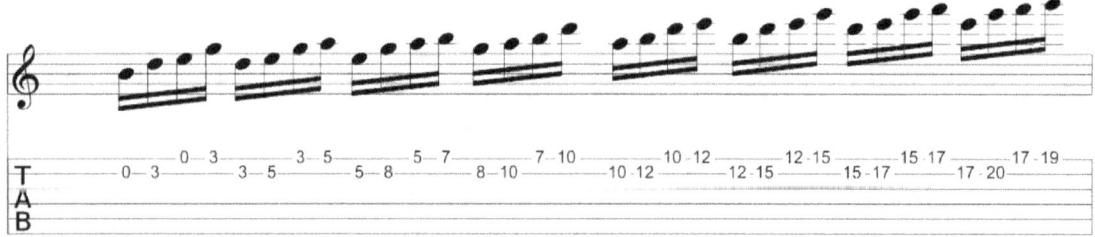

Pattern 4   Pattern 5   etc.

Moving Patterns To Other Strings

The pattern <u>order</u> is always the same but can start from different places.

On the D and G strings, the pattern sequence starts on Pattern 5.

E Minor Pentatonic D + G Strings

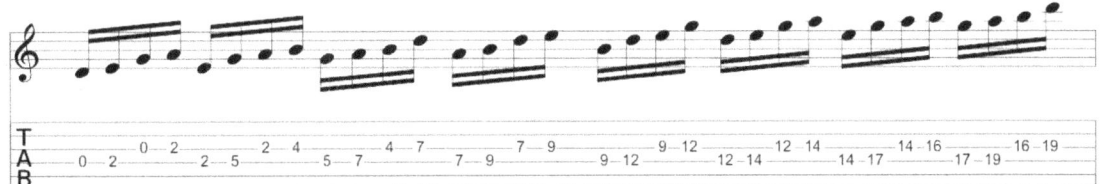

On the E and A strings, the pattern sequence starts on Pattern 1.

E Minor Pentatonic E + A Strings

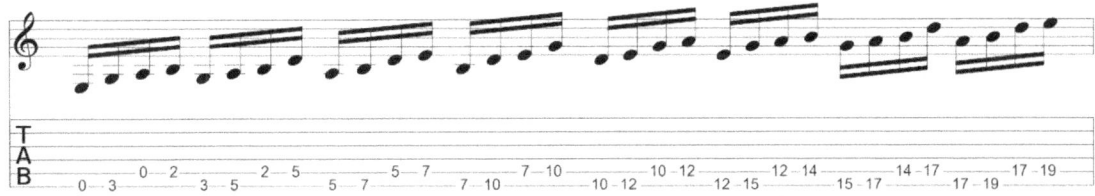

Pentatonic Positional Breakdown

Check this out! If the previous two-string patterns start on the low E string, D string or B string, the same pattern sequence can be used across the fretboard!

Here's the initial two-note-per-string pentatonic form:

E Minor Pentatonic: XII Position

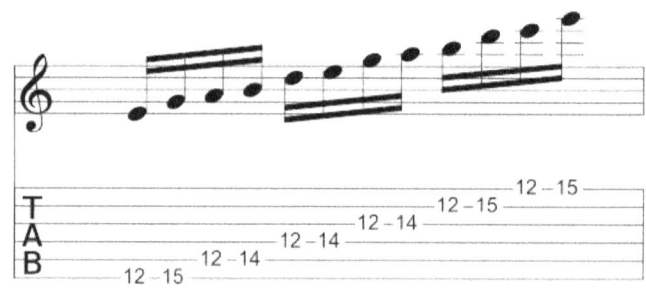

The two-string pattern starting on the E and A strings is Pattern 1.

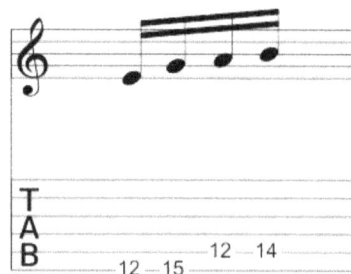

The pattern on the D and G strings is Pattern 5.

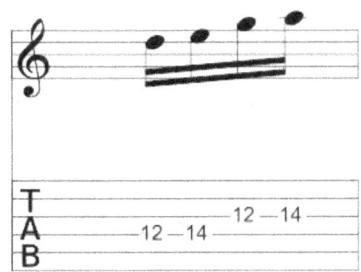

The pattern on the B and E strings is Pattern 4.

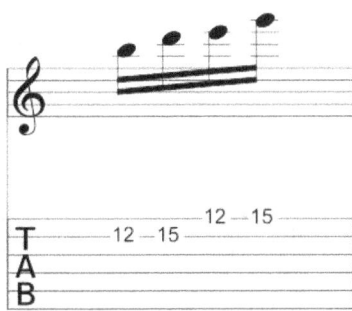

In other words, as you <u>ASCEND</u> in pitch across the strings,
the two-string patterns <u>DESCEND</u> by number.

This is true of ANY two-string pattern.

Using this two-string interlocking pattern idea, I'll demonstrate all of the positional pentatonic fingerings of E minor starting with the open position.

Two-String Horizontal (Positional) Patterns

E Minor Pentatonic: Open Position

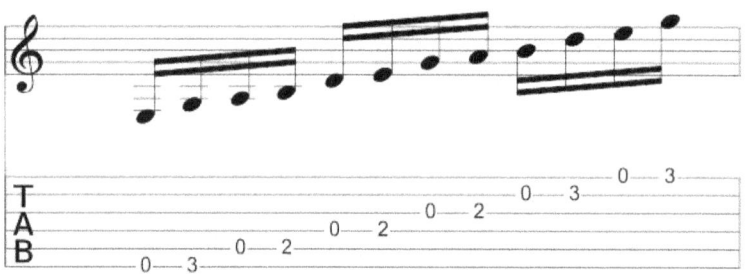

E Minor Pentatonic: 3rd Position

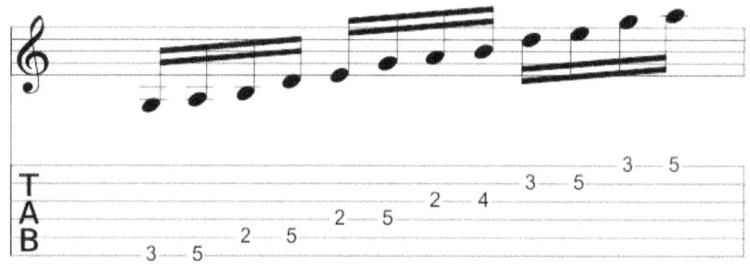

E Minor Pentatonic: 5th Position

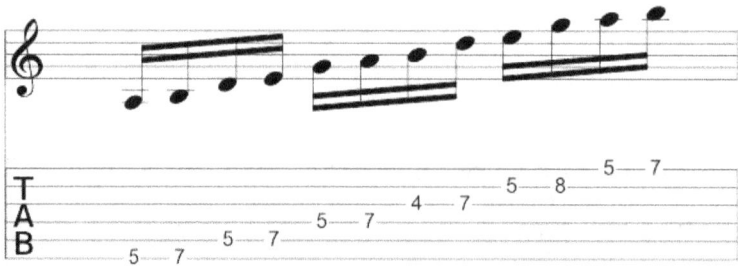

E Minor Pentatonic: 7th Position

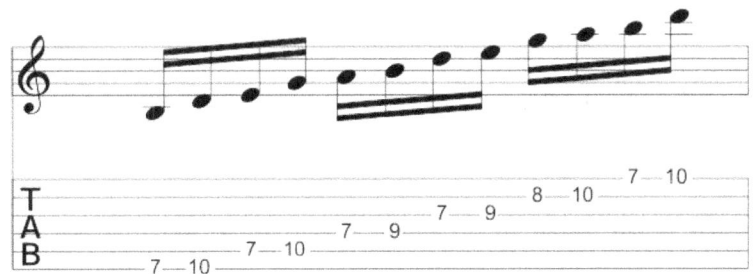

E Minor Pentatonic: 10th Position

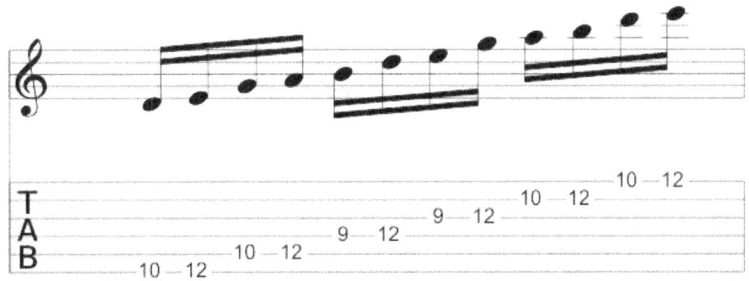

Again, the big points to remember here are:

As you *ascend* a scale in position
the patterns *descend* across two-string sets.

As you *descend* a scale in position
the patterns *ascend* across two-string sets.

For now, just work on getting the patterns under your fingers and associating the sounds with those fingering patterns so you can access them instantly.

Diagonal Forms - Part One

Playing a two-string pattern in octaves moves the fingering shape both horizontally *and* vertically (i.e. diagonally) across the fretboard. Two-string diagonal playing can help with visualization as the same pattern is simply moved to the same starting pitch but either one octave lower or higher.

I'll start with the two-string shapes we've looked at already to illustrate this. With the exception of the first four notes of the first pattern, which use open position, the rest of the patterns use the same fingering.

All of the following examples should be practiced with strict alternate picking or legato (i.e. using hammer-ons and pull offs) and (ideally) played over a chord to supply a harmonic context.

Diagonal Pattern #1 (in octaves)

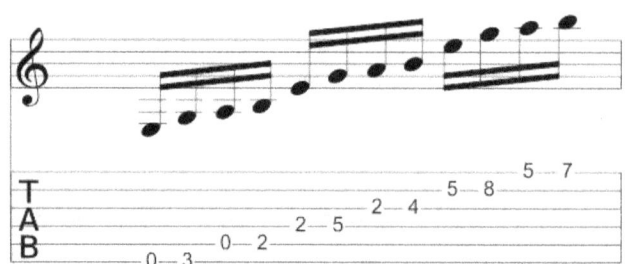

Diagonal Pattern # 2

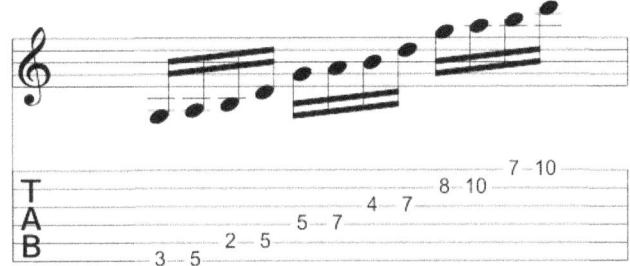

Diagonal Pattern # 3

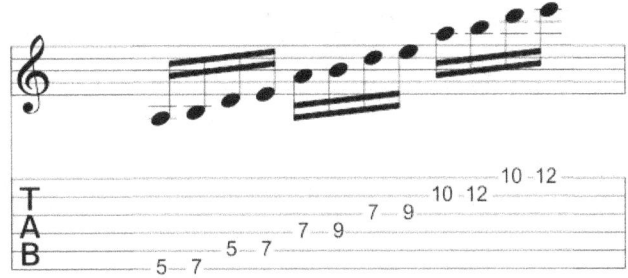

Diagonal Pattern # 4

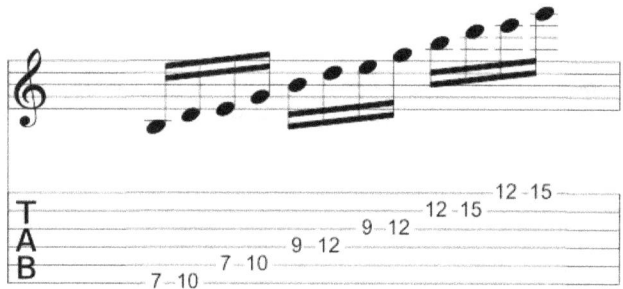

24

Diagonal Pattern # 5

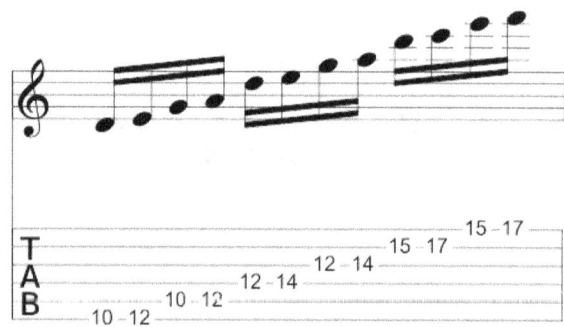

Working With Patterns

It's important to note that any scale is simply a tool in making music and isn't music in and of itself. The goal of this approach is to use these shapes as a way to visualize sounds and, ultimately, to be able to manipulate them in real-time to start making some music with them!

Let's generate a musical line using this approach. Here's an idea in the style of Paul Gilbert that uses hammer-ons and pull offs for a more legato feel (but you could pick every note to make the phrase more aggressive).

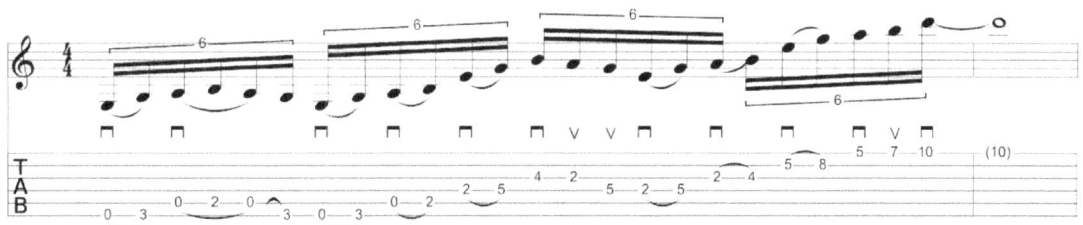

25

There are several ideas here worth exploiting.

- The initial pattern, consisting of four notes, is played as sextuplets (groups of six). This adds a rhythmic tension that's absent in phrasing the group of four notes into a 1/16th note pattern.

In general, practice playing patterns in a variety of rhythms as you may uncover additional ideas you can use later.

- The B on beat three breaks up the predictable note order a little. It's a small variation on the pattern that makes it sound a little less "patternish".

- The last five notes of the sextuplet break the four note melodic pattern. For ease of reading, I've notated it as a group of 5 in the examples below.

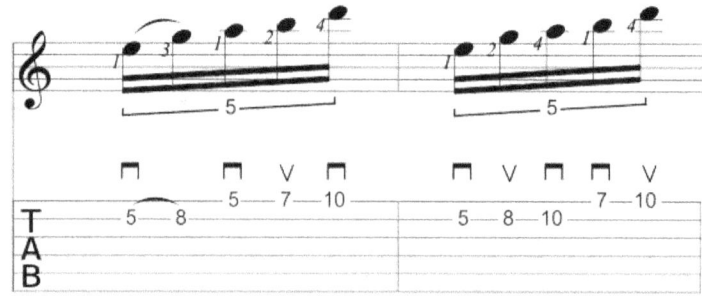

The use of the open E and A strings changes the overall fingering shape on the bottom, middle and top two strings which may make the lick more challenging to play.

TIP: If you have difficulty playing something melodically, take a close look at your fingering to see if it's the most efficient one.

In the example below, I've taken the notes from the previous example and broken them up into melodic shapes that use the G, A and B pitches on the same string.

You will probably find this much easier to play (but watch the skip from G to B on the D string!)

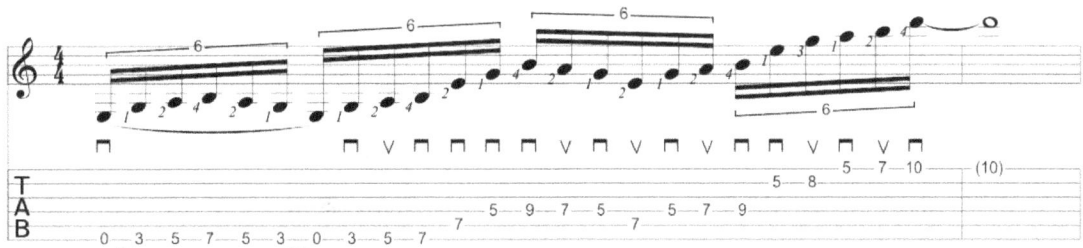

By understanding the fingerboard logic behind patterns, it becomes possible to manipulate them and make them work for you.

Sometimes patterns can lead us to unexpected melodic places as can be seen by an improvised variation on this idea on the following page.

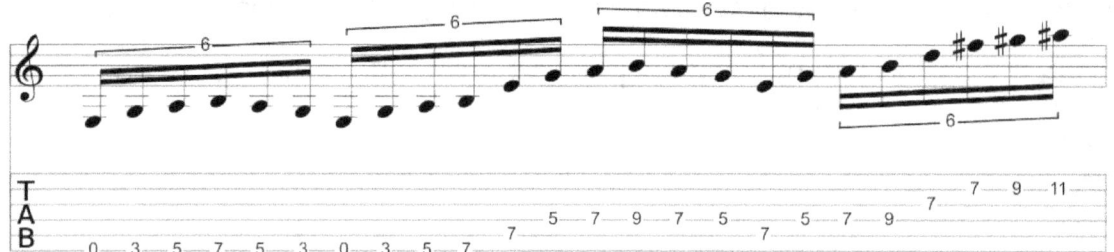

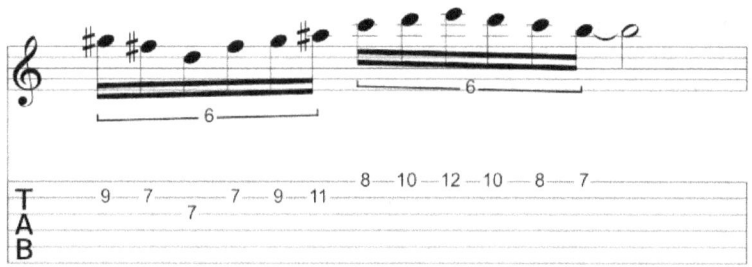

In this example, I've taken the initial fingerboard shape of the E, G, A and B pattern and instead of moving it up a 1/2 step, (to accommodate the B/G string 3rds tuning), I've kept the fingering shape the same.

The whole tone shape on the B string adds a melodic surprise and continues on the high E string (before resolving it to B). The whole steps between the F♯, G♯ and A♯ and the C, D and E provide a melodic continuity with the G, A and B of the E minor pentatonic scale.

Even though the G♯ clashes with the G in E minor - the line has enough of a melodic drive that it can work <u>as long as you resolve the idea</u> (in this case to a chord tone).

28

Diagonal Forms - Part Two

Now let's examine five-note patterns on two strings in more depth. There are generally two positional variations of these patterns that can be employed. The first uses two notes on one string and three on another (i.e. a 2-3 pattern):

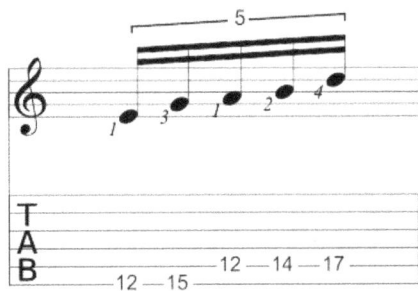

The second variation is a 3-2 pattern:

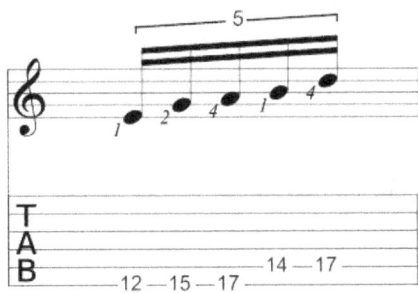

From a picking perspective - I find the 3-2 pattern typically works best when ascending and the 2-3 works best when descending. In terms of fingering, the reverse of this will often be true but as with everything presented here, use what works for you!

Each of the individual shapes (with some personal observations) follow.

Five-Note Diagonal Pattern 1 (Starting on the Root)

Here are the 2-3 and the 3-2 patterns on the bottom two strings.

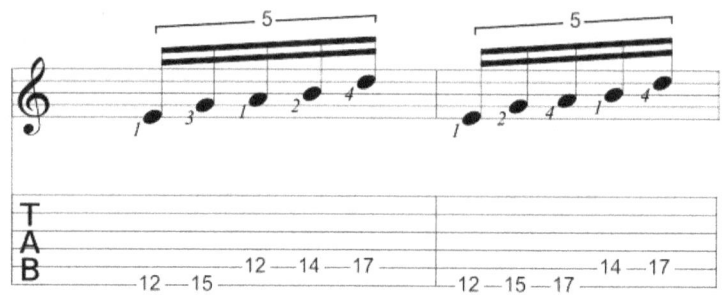

Here are the multi-octave variations.

30

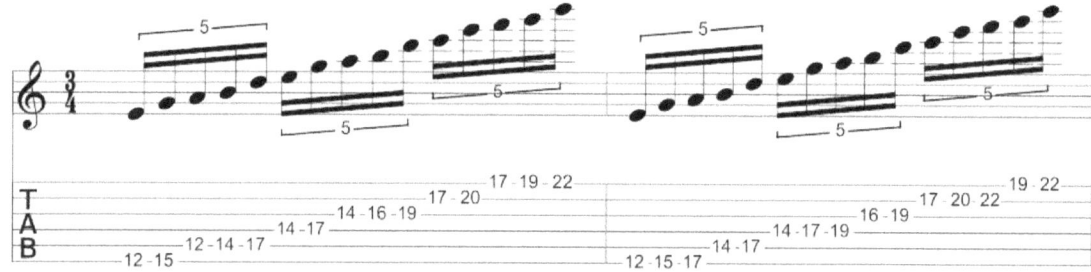

Since the pattern is five notes long, I've notated it as a rhythmic division of five in the examples above, but it can be practiced with a variety of rhythms. Here I've notated it as both septuplets and as 1/16th notes.

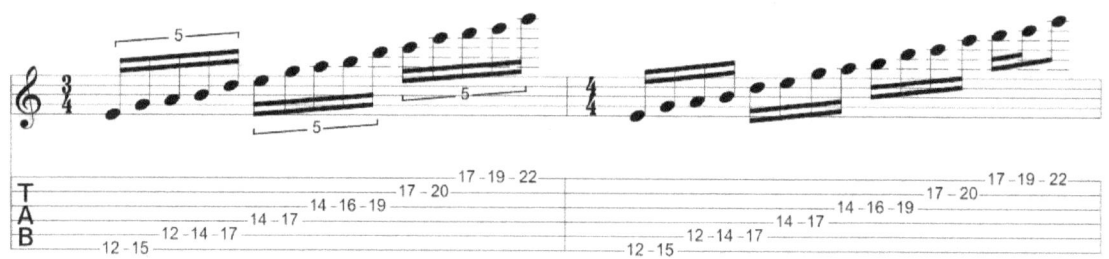

Five-Note Diagonal Pattern 2 (Starting on the ♭3rd)

The 2-3 pattern doesn't sit very well under my fingers when played ascending so I use it primarily for descending ideas.

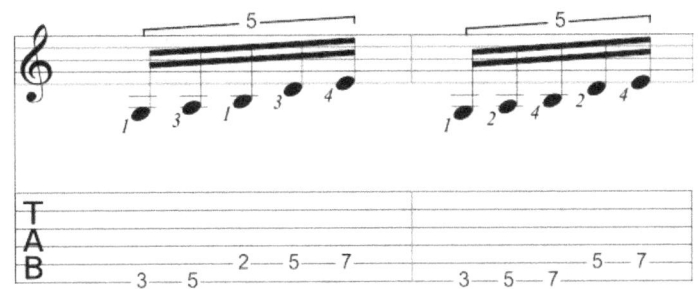

In contrast, the symmetrical fingering of the 2nd and 4th finger in the 3-2 pattern is more ergonomic to me. I'm not a big proponent of finger exercises, but if you're looking for a fingering pattern to clean up your 2nd and 4th finger synchronization, smoothing out the octave runs on this shape will help (if you're practicing it correctly).

Here are the multi-octave versions.

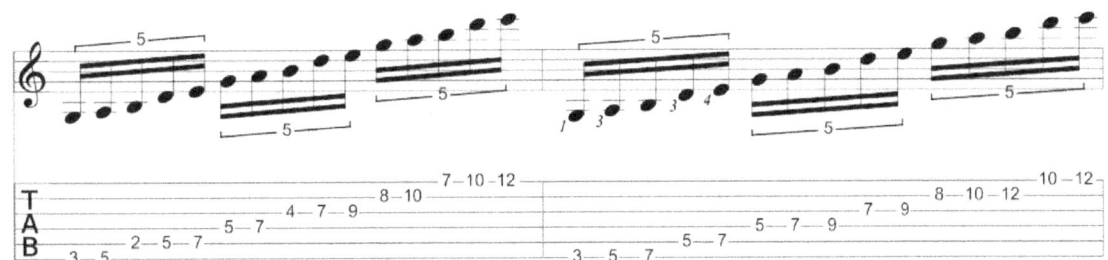

Five-Note Diagonal Pattern 3 (Starting on the 4th)

In this instance, I prefer the 2-3 pattern to the 3-2 shape as I find that the repetition of the first and second fingers to be more comfortable than repeating the use of the second and fourth fingers.

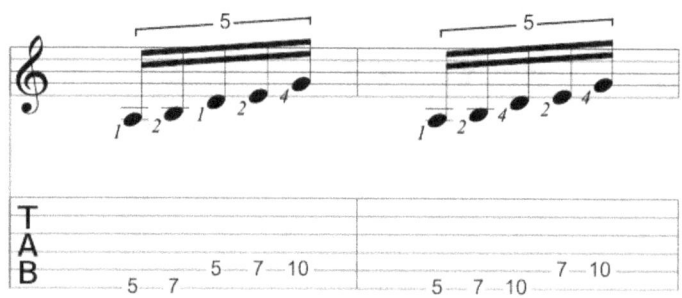

Here are the multi-octave versions. I play the 2-3 pattern **primarily** with alternate picking, but play two down strokes in a row to get from the G to the A. This allows me to start every two-string pattern on a down stroke.

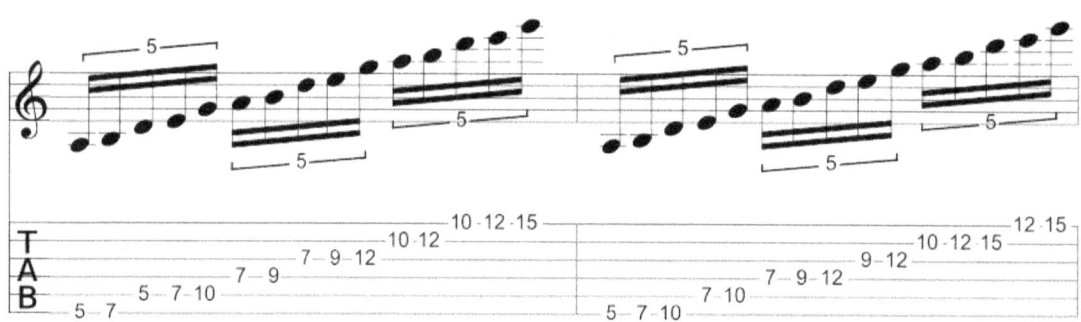

Five-Note Diagonal Pattern 4 (Starting on the 5th)

As with the previous example, most guitarists will prefer the 2-3 pattern as it uses the first and third fingers instead of the third and fourth fingers.

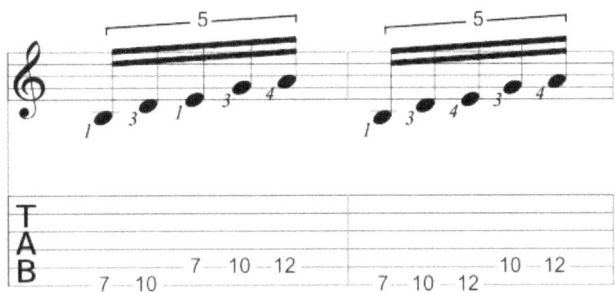

For the multi-octave version, I use the same picking pattern described in Pattern 3 for this pattern.

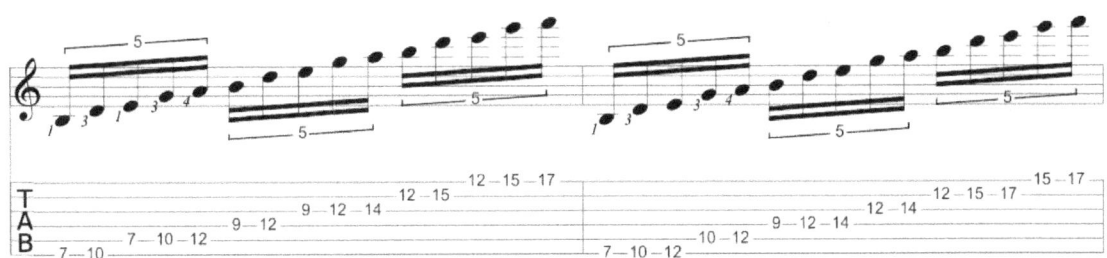

Five-Note Diagonal Pattern 5 (Starting on the ♭7th)

Since the 2-3 pattern sits under my fingers very comfortably, the 3-2 pattern is a form I abandoned almost instantly.

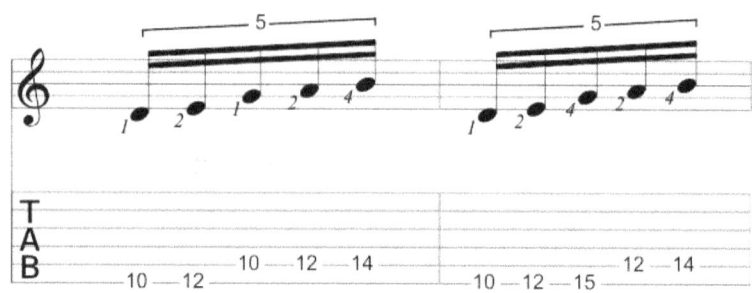

Played in octaves, the 2-3 is a great shape to repeat a few times before moving to the next octave and the 3-2 pattern can be useful when *descending*.

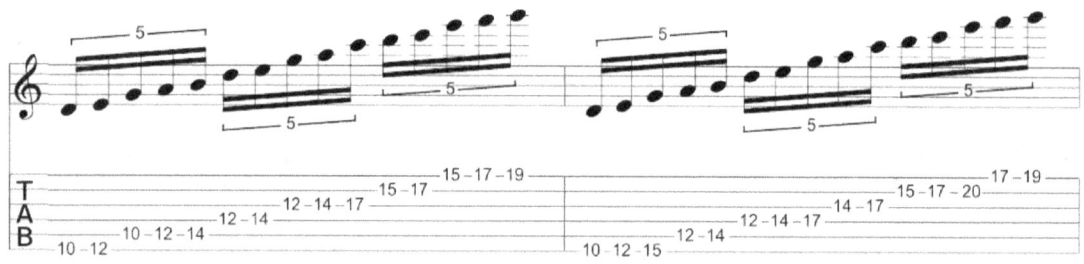

Note: These shapes are all adaptable to the blues scale as well by just adding the note A♯/B♭ to the patterns.

Section II:

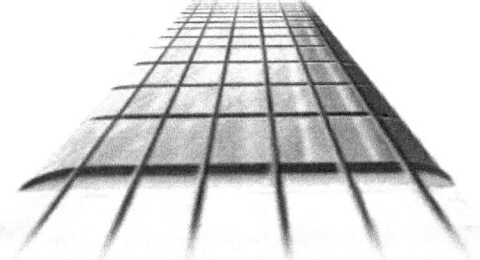

Using The Minor Pentatonic Scale

Tonal Center Analysis

The chart below presents E Minor Pentatonic in relation to every note of the chromatic scale as a tonal center. Note: If the terms in the chart don't make sense, you may want to read the chord/interval theory primer/review section of the book starting on page 83.

Tonal Center	E Minor Pentatonic				
	E	G	A	B	D
E	R	♭3	11	5	♭7
F	7	9	3	♯11	13
F♯ / G♭	♭7	♭9	♭3/ ♯9	11	♭13/ ♯5
G	13	R	9	3	5
G♯ / A♭	♭13	7	♭9	♭3/ ♯9	♭5/♯11
A	5	♭7	R	9	11
A♯ / B♭	♭5/♯11	13	7	♭9	3
B	11	♭13	♭7	R	♭3
C	3	5	13	7	9
C♯ /D♭	♭3/ ♯9	♭5/♯11	♭13	♭7	♭9
D	9	11	5	13	R
D♯ /E♭	♭9	3	♭5/♯11	♭13	7

36

From this, some general shortcuts can be applied to using any minor pentatonic scale over various harmonic contexts. While this is by no means a complete list of applications, it's comprehensive enough to act as a launching point for your own sonic explorations.

Major Chords

Over a major chord: try playing minor pentatonics from the 3rd, 6th or 7th scale degree.

For example, over a C Major chord you could play:

E	Minor Pentatonic
A	Minor Pentatonic
B	Minor Pentatonic

C Major (C Major, Major 7)				

E Minor Pentatonic	E	G	A	B	D
	3	5	13	7	9

A Minor Pentatonic	A	C	D	E	G
	6	R	9	3	5

B Minor Pentatonic	B	D	E	C	A
	7	9	3	R	13

Minor Chords

Over a minor chord, try playing a minor pentatonic based on the Root, 2nd or 5th scale degree.

Over an E minor chord you could play:

E	Minor Pentatonic
F♯	Minor Pentatonic
B	Minor Pentatonic

E minor
(E min, E minor 7)

E Minor Pentatonic	E	G	A	B	D
	R	♭3	11	5	7

F# Minor Pentatonic	F#	A	B	C♯	E
	2	11	5	13	R

B Minor Pentatonic	B	D	E	F♯	A
	5	7	R	9	13

Dominant 7th Chords

Over a dominant 7th chord or a 7 (sus4) chord - try playing a minor pentatonic from the Root, 2nd , 5th or 6th scale degree.

Over an E7 or E7(sus) chord you could play:

E	Minor Pentatonic
F#	Minor Pentatonic
B	Minor Pentatonic
C#	Minor Pentatonic

E7 or E7(sus)					

E Minor Pentatonic	E	G	A	B	D
	R	#9	11	5	♭7

F# Minor Pentatonic	F#	A	B	C#	E
	9	11	5	13	R

B Minor Pentatonic	B	D	E	F#	A
	5	♭7	R	9	11

C# Minor Pentatonic	C#	E	F#	G#	B
	13	R	9	3	5

Altered Dominant 7ᵗʰ (Alt) Chords

Over an altered dominant chord (altered extensions are ♭5, ♯5, ♭9, ♯9), try playing a minor pentatonic from the ♭3ʳᵈ, 4ᵗʰ or ♭7ᵗʰ scale degree.

Over a E altered dominant chord you could play:

G	Minor Pentatonic
A	Minor Pentatonic
D	Minor Pentatonic

E alt

G Minor Pentatonic	G	B♭	C	D	F
	♯9*	♭5	♯5*	♭7	♭9

A Minor Pentatonic	A	C	D	E	G
	11	♯5*	♭7	R	♯9*

D Minor Pentatonic	D	F	G	A	C
	♭7	♭9	♯9*	11	♯5*

* Note: Enharmonically a ♭3 is the same as a ♯9. In the key of E, F♯ is a 9ᵗʰ so sharping that 9 (i.e. raising it a ½ step) makes it F♯♯ aka G). In the same way, a ♭6 is enharmonically the same as a ♯5. While G is a ♭3 in the key of E it's written as a ♯9 to show how it fits in an altered chord.

Sample Chord Progressions

In Jazz soloing, one mode of thinking is to change the scale each time you change the chord. Having said that, considerable melodic mileage can come from squeezing whatever you can out of a single scale. So let me offer a few broad ideas that may help you with using the pentatonic minor scale.

It bears repeating that just because you *can* use a melodic device doesn't always mean that you *should*. The success of any of the applications recommended here is ultimately going to depend on the musicality of the performer!

II-V-I

One of the most commonly used progressions in Jazz is the II V→ I (in the key of C: D min7 G7 → C Major 7). You can use a minor pentatonic a 3rd above the I chord to solo over the whole phrase (i.e. E Minor Pentatonic over a II V → I in C). It's a very distinct sound and one that won't work for too long over multiple choruses of a song, but it is a useable device.

Diatonic Major

To extend this idea a little further, since E Minor Pentatonic doesn't contain any avoid notes in the key of C, you can use it over *any* diatonic chord progression in C Major.

Melodic Minor

As a general rule, a minor pentatonic scale a step above the root of a melodic minor scale can work over any chord in the melodic minor scale (and thus any chord progression in Melodic Minor). E Minor Pentatonic can then be played over any chord (or diatonic chord progression) in D Melodic Minor. (D min (maj 7), E min 7, F maj 7(#5), G7, A7, B min7♭5 and C# min 7♭5)! Some of these sounds are definitely not for everyone, but this approach may open some new doorways in your hearing and playing!

Minor Chord Vamps A Step Away

In an E min7 – D Min7 vamp, you can play E Minor Pentatonic over the whole thing (though whether on not you'll want to after three to four passes is a different matter entirely!)

To sum up, E Minor Pentatonic will work over:

- C major / C major 7

- G major / G major 7 / G7

- F major / F major 7 / F maj 7 (#5)

- E min / E min 7

- A min / A min 7 / A7

- D min / D min 7 / D min (maj 7) / D7

- B Alt / B min 7♭5

- C# min 7♭5

The Blues Scale

I find the minor pentatonic to have more harmonic possibilities than the blues scale but you could just add the tritone (♯4 or ♭5) to the pentatonic patterns I've covered and they'll still interlock across the fingerboard in the same way.

The Major Pentatonic Scale

The notes in E Minor Pentatonic are the same as those in G Major Pentatonic. **When playing over major tonalities, rather than thinking of major pentatonic fingerings, I play minor pentatonic patterns from the relative minor scale over them.** For example, instead of playing a C Major Pentatonic over a C Major tonality I use A Minor Pentatonic patterns to get the same result.

Section III:

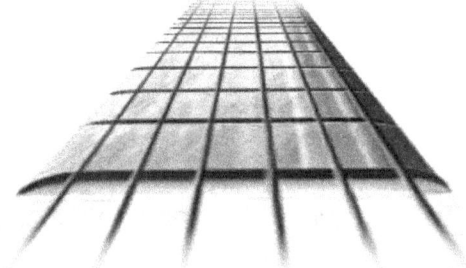

Breaking Out Of The Box

Two-Note Single String Patterns

One way to break out of the box position involves looking at pentatonic scales as single-string scales that can be visualized on the fingerboard vertically (i.e. up and down).   Playing E Minor Pentatonic on the top two strings produces <u>five</u> two-note patterns:

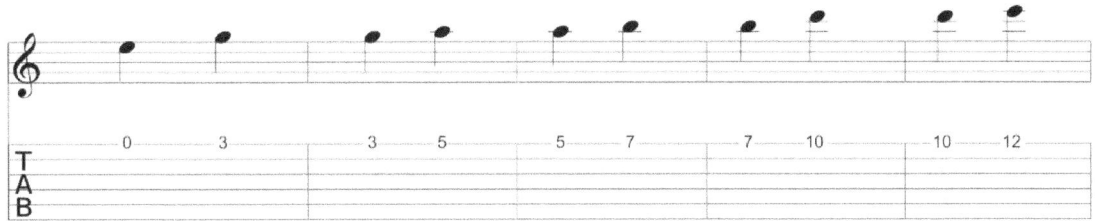

Here's the same scale repeating the first pattern at the 12th fret.

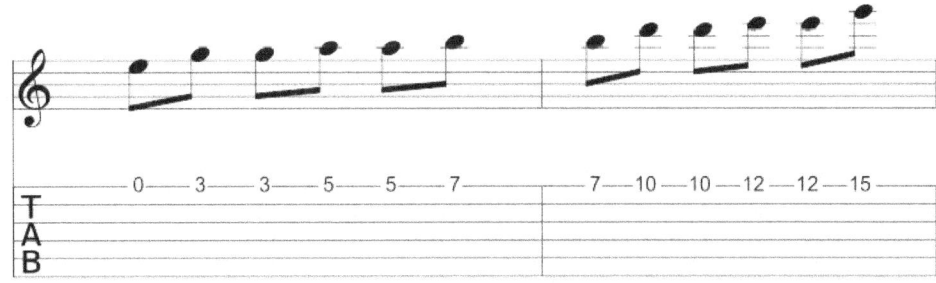

Since all of the open strings of the guitar in standard tuning are notes in the E Minor Pentatonic scale, I'll repeat this with the other strings.

E Minor Pentatonic on the B string starts with the fourth pattern.

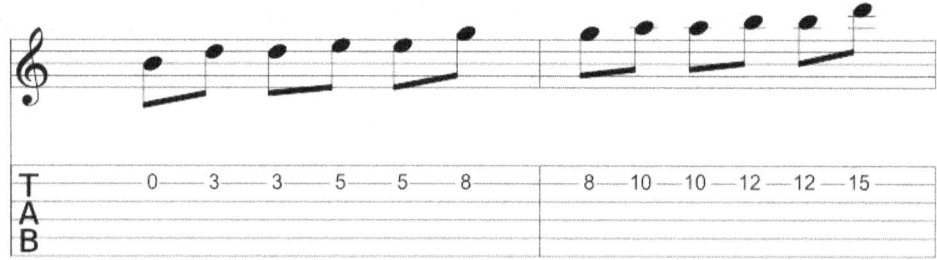

E Minor Pentatonic on the G string starts with the second pattern.

46

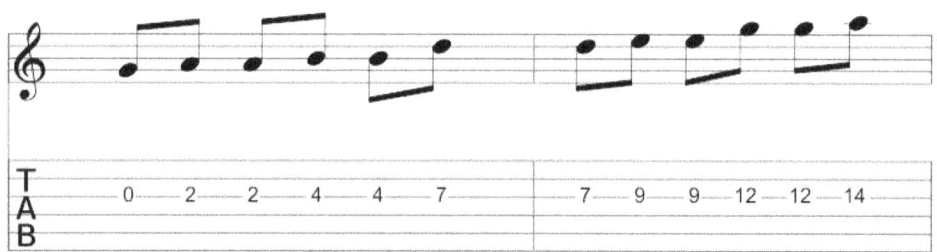

The E Minor Pentatonic on the D string starts with the fifth pattern.

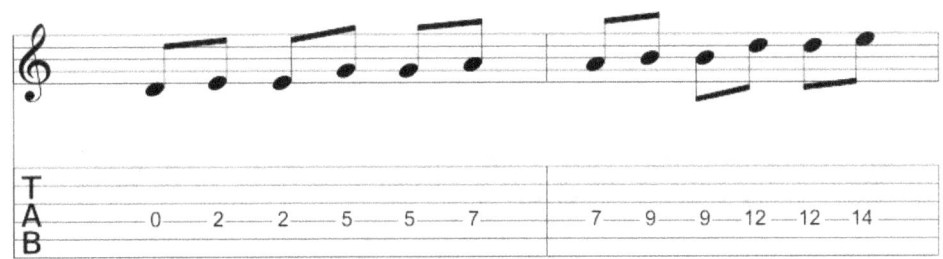

The E Minor Pentatonic on the A string starts with the third pattern.

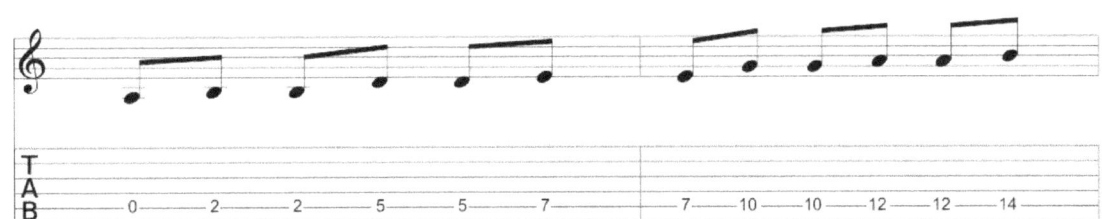

Finally, the patterns on the low E string are the same as the high E string.

Once two-string patterns are visualized, mixing and matching the patterns on different strings open up a number of harmonic possibilities.

For example, as the tuning of the guitar creates a 9th between the A and the B string alternating between the two can create some interesting ideas. Here, the patterns are simply played as an ascending idea:

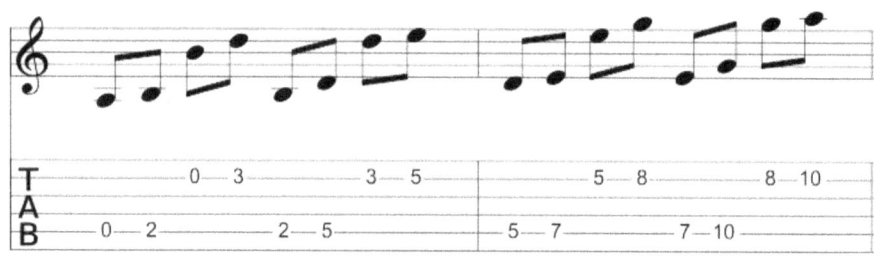

Here's a variation of the same idea that ascends one string at a time:

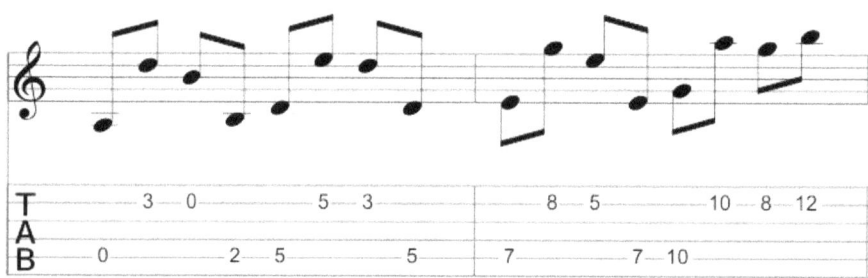

Here, this approach exploits the 9th between the D and E string:

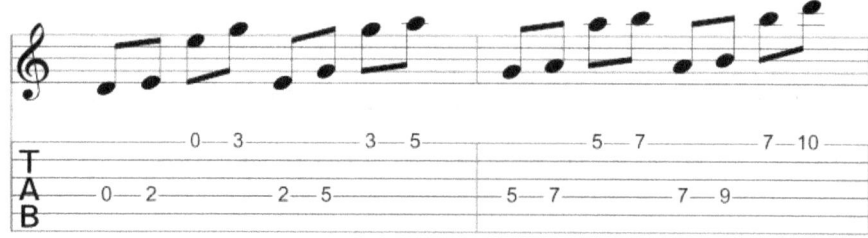

It can also be adapted to the 7th between the A and G strings.

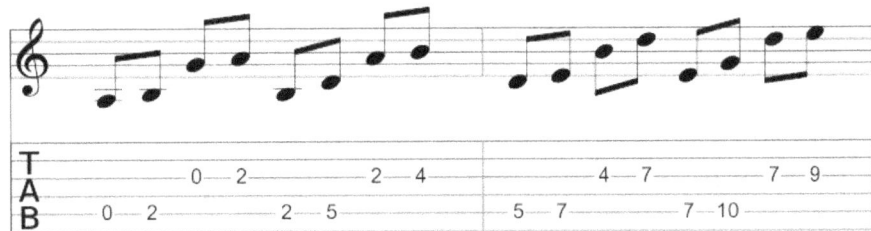

The G and E strings often work really well in generating some interesting melodic ideas. In this example, I've use the starting note of every two-note pattern to generate a wide-interval ascending pattern.

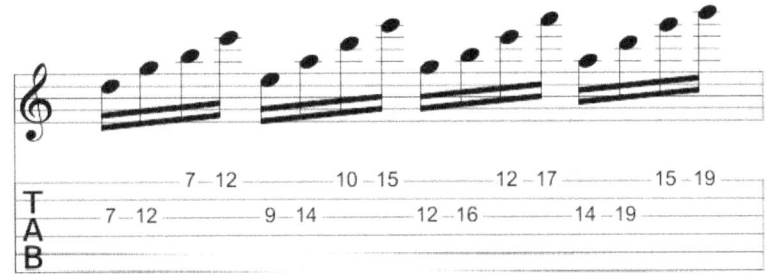

Be careful of those stretches! If you feel any pain when playing them, stop immediately!

Another way to break out of the box is to start visualizing these patterns as three-note shapes.

Three-Note Single String Patterns

Playing E Minor Pentatonic as a series of three-note patterns that star from each scale degree on the high E-string looks like this:

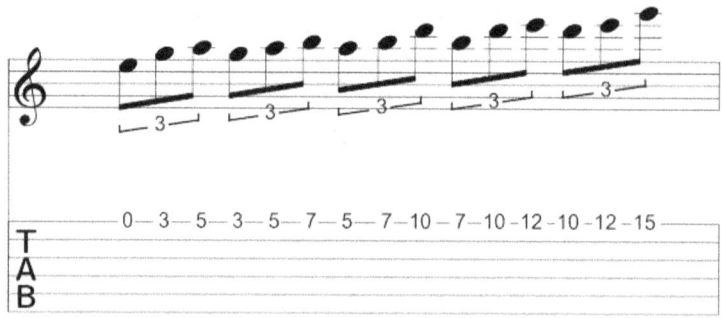

Here's the scale moved to the B string.

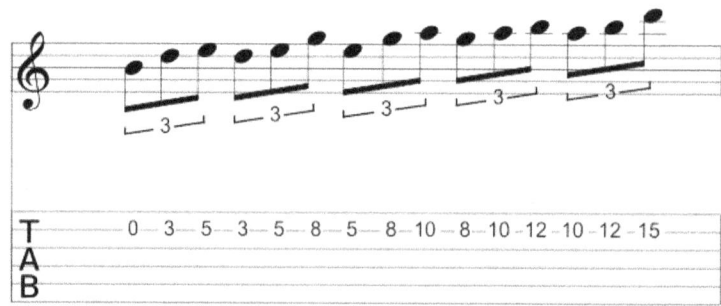

Here it's played on the G string.

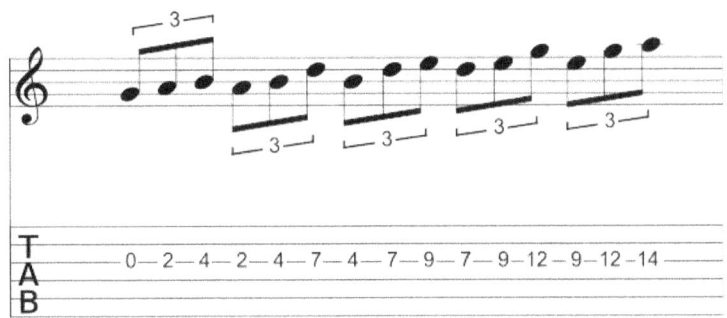

Played on the D string.

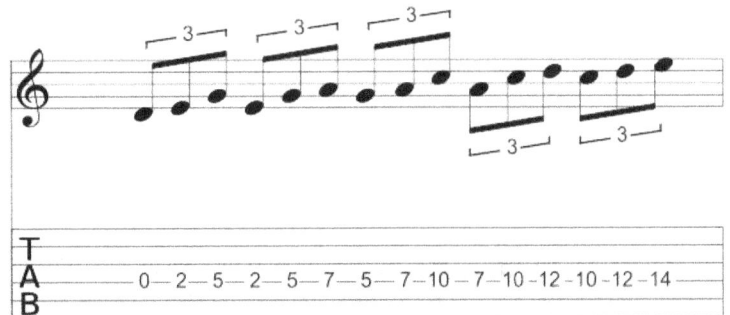

Played on the A string.

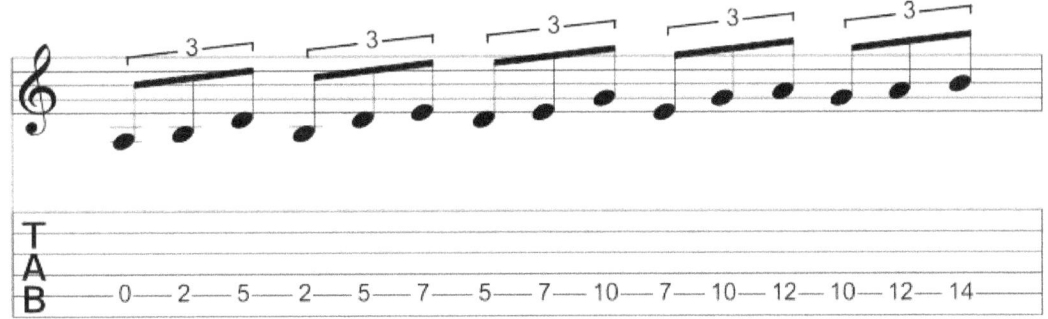

The same ideas that were employed with the two-note patterns can be applied here. While I've outlined a few additional pattern ideas below, my *Melodic Patterns* book employs <u>thousands</u> of systematic variations that cover this topic much more thoroughly than I can here.

The following examples utilize some wide stretches on the G and E strings. Like the two-note patterns, if you feel any discomfort, stop immediately!

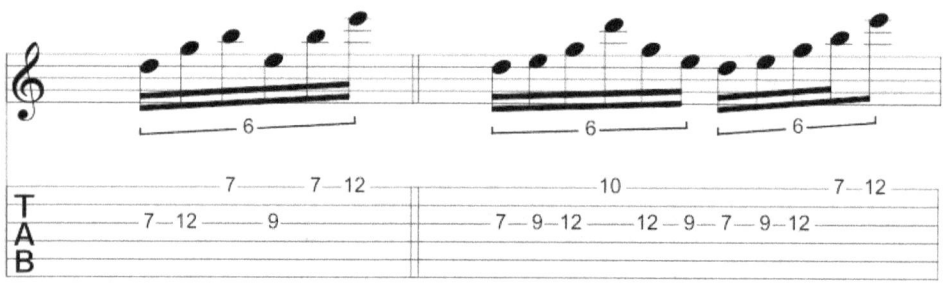

This next example employs a string skip that only uses three unique shapes. Playing it cleanly will take no small amount of practice but if you practice it slowly with proper technique and really focus on the articulation and timing of the notes, speed will be a natural byproduct eventually.

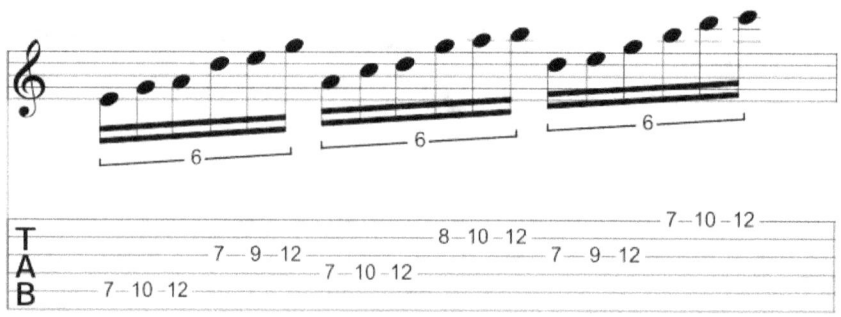

Note-Per-String Patterns For All Six Strings

The following material deals with breaking out of the two-string patterns examined so far. Since many licks are visual (i.e. associated with certain patterns or areas of the fingerboard), having multiple ways to view fingering options is beneficial. Additionally, certain melodic and harmonic ideas will be easier to play on different string sets.

If we look at a fingering for E Minor Pentatonic (and each string uses two notes of the pattern per string), it can be written as 2-2-2-2-2-2.

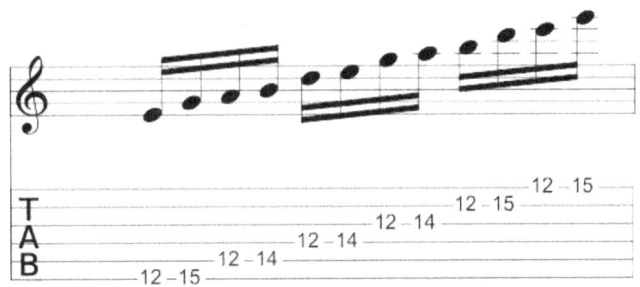

53

To find different fingering ideas we can simply examine other note-per-string fingering options. For example:

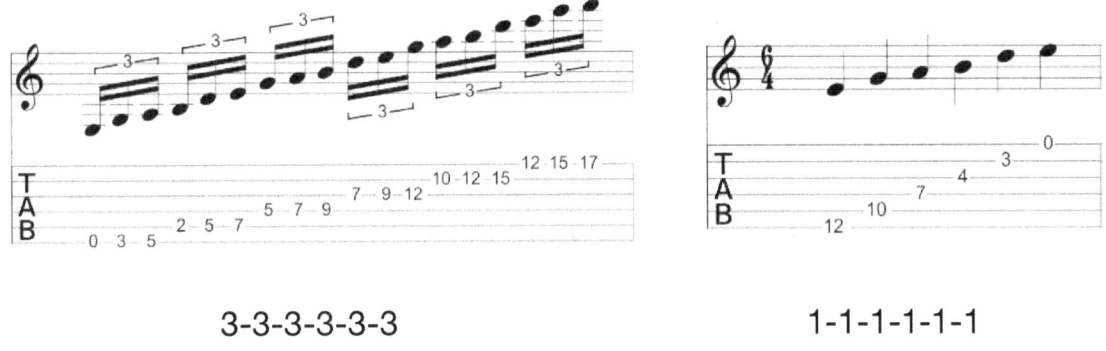

3-3-3-3-3-3   1-1-1-1-1-1

A chart on page 92 shows all theoretical variations of this approach but there has been one particular variation (1-3-1-3-1-3) that has opened the most doors in my own playing.

Sweep Picking The Minor Pentatonic Scale

There are largest advantage to the (1-3-1-3-1-3) fingering is that it facilitates *sweep picking* the scale. While sweep picking (i.e. two or more pick strokes in the same direction on adjacent strings) is typically associated with arpeggios, in this case it can be used to play scalar passages more efficiently.

Rather than simply show the patterns, I'll demonstrate how I derived them so you can apply the idea to any other pentatonic (or two-note-per-string fingering). The following examples use the B Minor Pentatonic scale and while it can be played over a B minor chord, to my ears it works even better over an E min, E min 7 or E min 9 chord.

54

To review, here is B Minor Pentatonic starting from the root in 7th position.

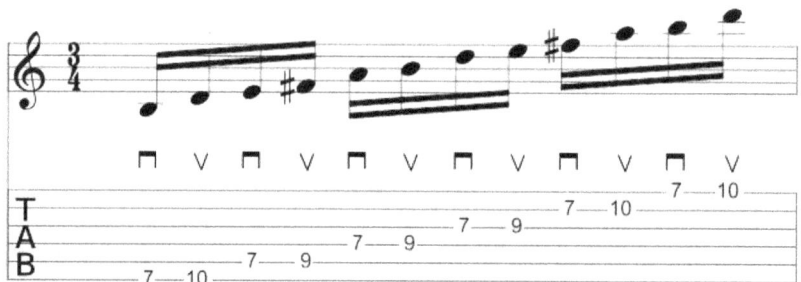

Since this is being played over an E minor tonality, I'm going to start the scale from the E note on the A string and then add an E on the 12th fret of the high E string.

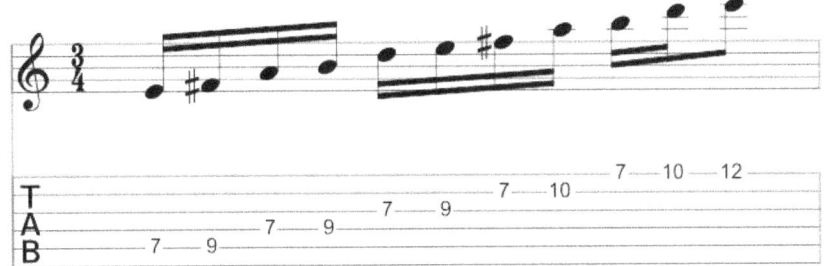

Two-note-per string patterns lend themselves well to alternate picking but don't work well for sweeping. To sweep pick this scale, I'll modify the number of notes per string from two to an odd number.

To start, I'll take the A on the D string and move it to the 12th fret of the A string. For all the examples presented here, play any notes on the 7th fret with the first finger, 9th fret with the second finger, 10th fret with the third finger and any notes on the 11th or 12th fret with the pinky.

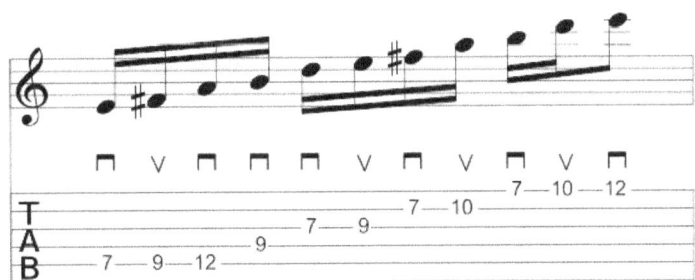

Also note: the stretches involved in some of these patterns may be too much for your level of flexibility. You can always transpose the pattern up (i.e. play the pattern where the frets are closer together) which makes it easier to play.

Note: If any of the stretches presented here are painful in any way you should stop immediately! You can do long term damage to yourself by practicing through pain!

Now I'll take the same approach and apply it to the other strings in this scale. Most guitarists typically use arpeggios with one note per string fingerings when using sweep picking. However, the three-notes-per-string fingering (alternating with a single note-per-string shape) creates a pattern that can be sweep picked quite efficiently.

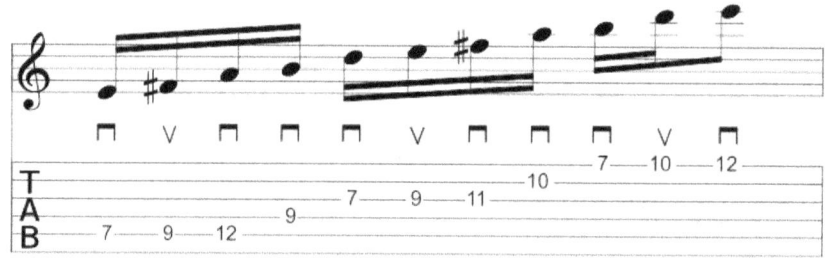

If you want to get a little more use out of this approach, switching the F♯ to G will create an E Minor Pentatonic scale:

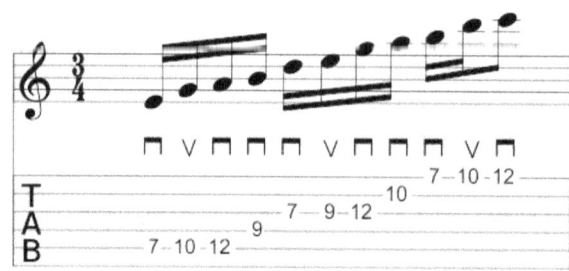

From there, switching any A with an A♯/B♭ will create an E Blues sweep.

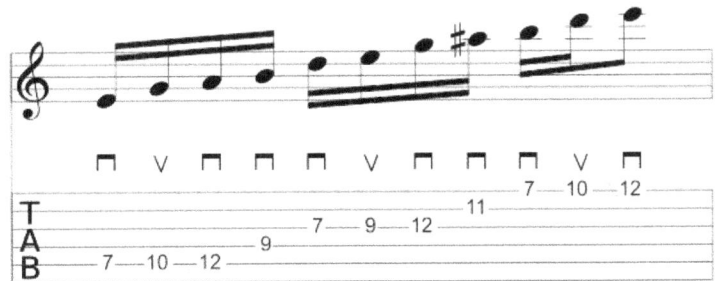

To descend the scale, simply use upstrokes on adjacent strings.

The most challenging part of this process for most people is getting the initial sweep down. The following repeating lick can help synchronize your hands and it sounds cool!

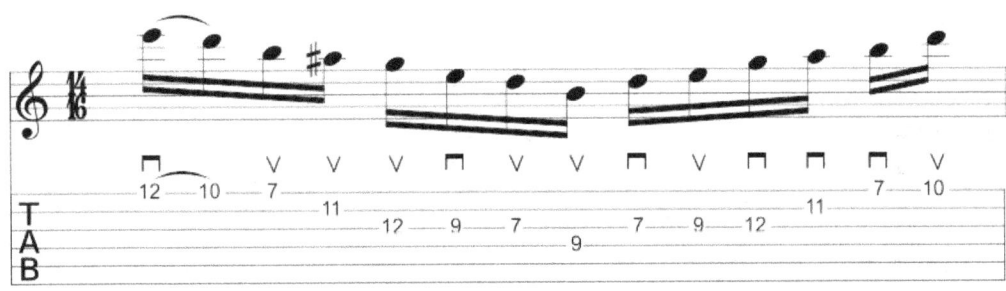

Don't worry about the time signature! Just play the notes in a consistent rhythm and the eighth repetition will land on a downbeat. (Here's a rhythm tip. Another way to think of 14/16 is to call it 7/4. If you play the phrase 7 times over a 4/4 pattern, the 8th time will land on the 1st beat of a 4/4 measure. This concept can be applied to other meters as well!

Examples

Example 1:

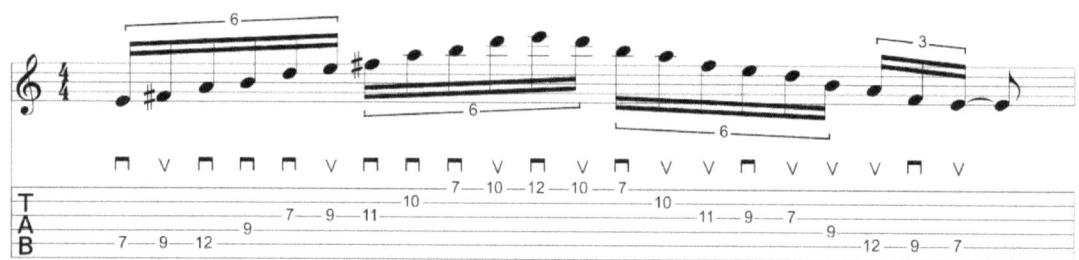

The next lick is a transcription of an improvised variation on the scale.

58

Example 2:

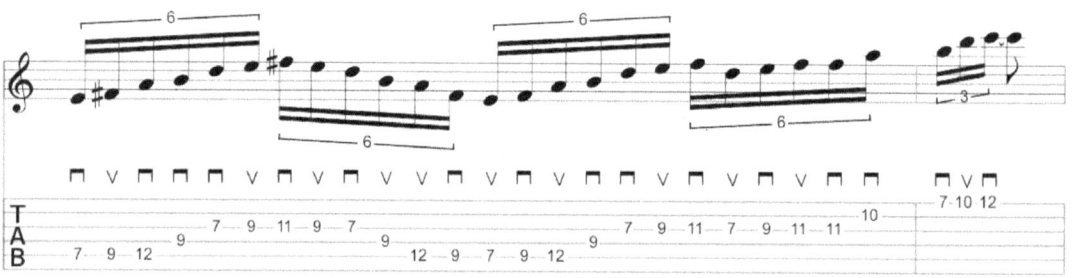

If you work with this approach for a while, the picking patterns will become automatic allowing you to focus more on the music and less on the actual technique.

Section IV:

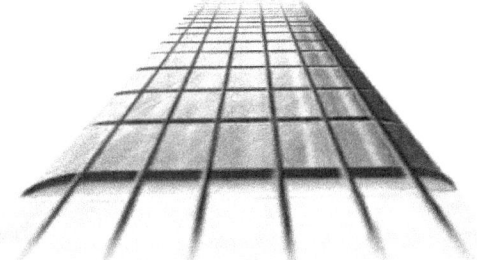

Breaking Into The Box

Breaking Into The Box

Sometimes the best way to break out of the box is to break into it. You can get new sounds out of a pentatonic scale just by varying the note order of the patterns your playing.

Every example explored here looks at playing the notes in a straight ascending order but it can be used for descending ideas as well. For instance, if I have the first five notes of E Minor Pentatonic:

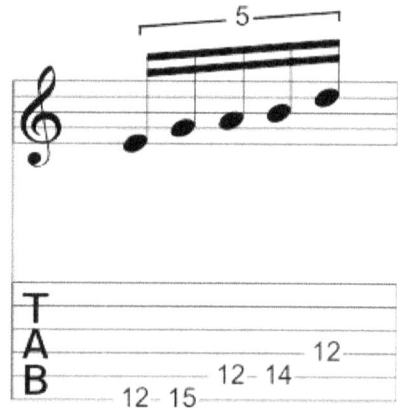

I can create a sequence from these notes by playing the same note order (1-2-3-4-5) starting from each scale degree like so:

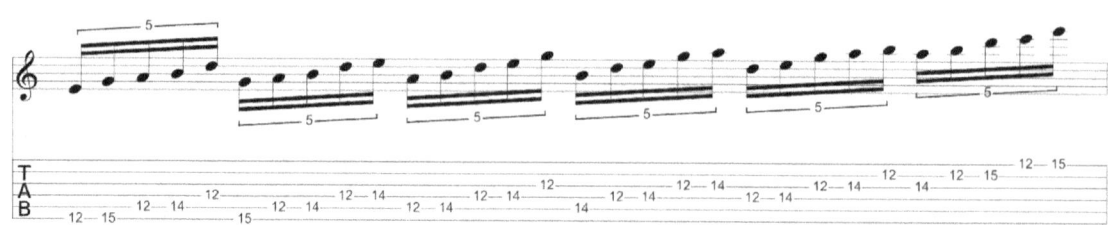

Changing the note order to 1-2-4-3-5 changes the initial pattern to this:

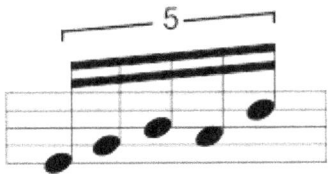

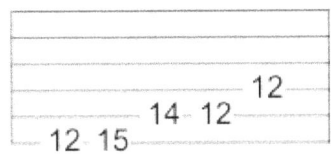

and completely alters the sound of the sequence produced.

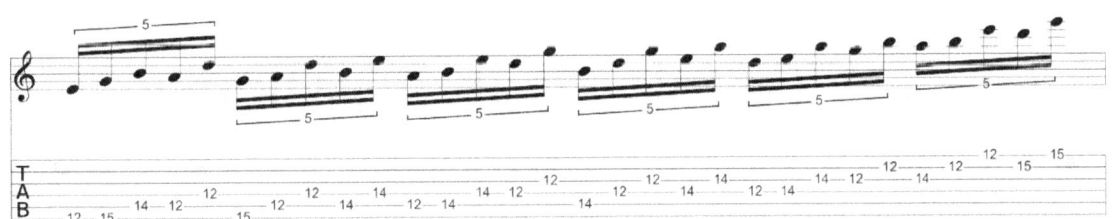

The chart on page 101 documents all of the possible five-note orders of any pentatonic scale. If you like this approach, you may want to check out my *Melodic Patterns* book which goes much deeper into this concept.

Section V:

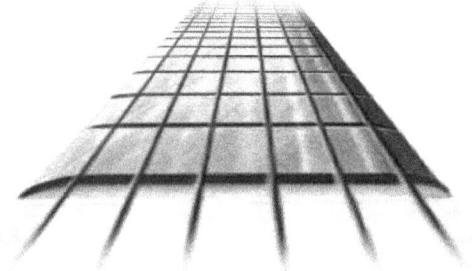

Pentatonic Harmonization

62

Pentatonic Harmony: Triads

E Minor Pentatonic/ G Major Pentatonic essentially harmonizes into two chords using the roots E and G:

E min 7 (add 11)   and   G 6/9

There are a number of other possible chords that can be implied from these notes depending on the tonic. I've included both the tonal center chart and a chord guide in this book to help determine other possible chords you could use it over. Since I tend to view things as larger harmonic systems, I try to find tonal centers that work for me and then apply voicings that make sense.

Viewed mathematically, a pentatonic scale can only have ten possible unique triads based on scale degree:

| 1,2,3 | 1,3,4 | 1,4,5 | 2,3,4 | 2,4,5 | 3,4,5 |

| 1,2,4 | 1,3,5 | | 2,3,5 |

| 1,2,5 |

Using E Minor Pentatonic as an example produces:

| E,G,A | E,A,B | E,B,D | G,A,B | G,B,D | A,B,D |

| E,G,B | E,A,D | | G,A,D |

| E,G,D |

I've tabbed out ONE notational possibility below which uses the 3rd between in G and B strings to get some cool sounding cluster chords. You should feel free to work out your own voicings of the notes based on what sounds good to you. These could either be played as a chord or played one note at a time as an arpeggio.

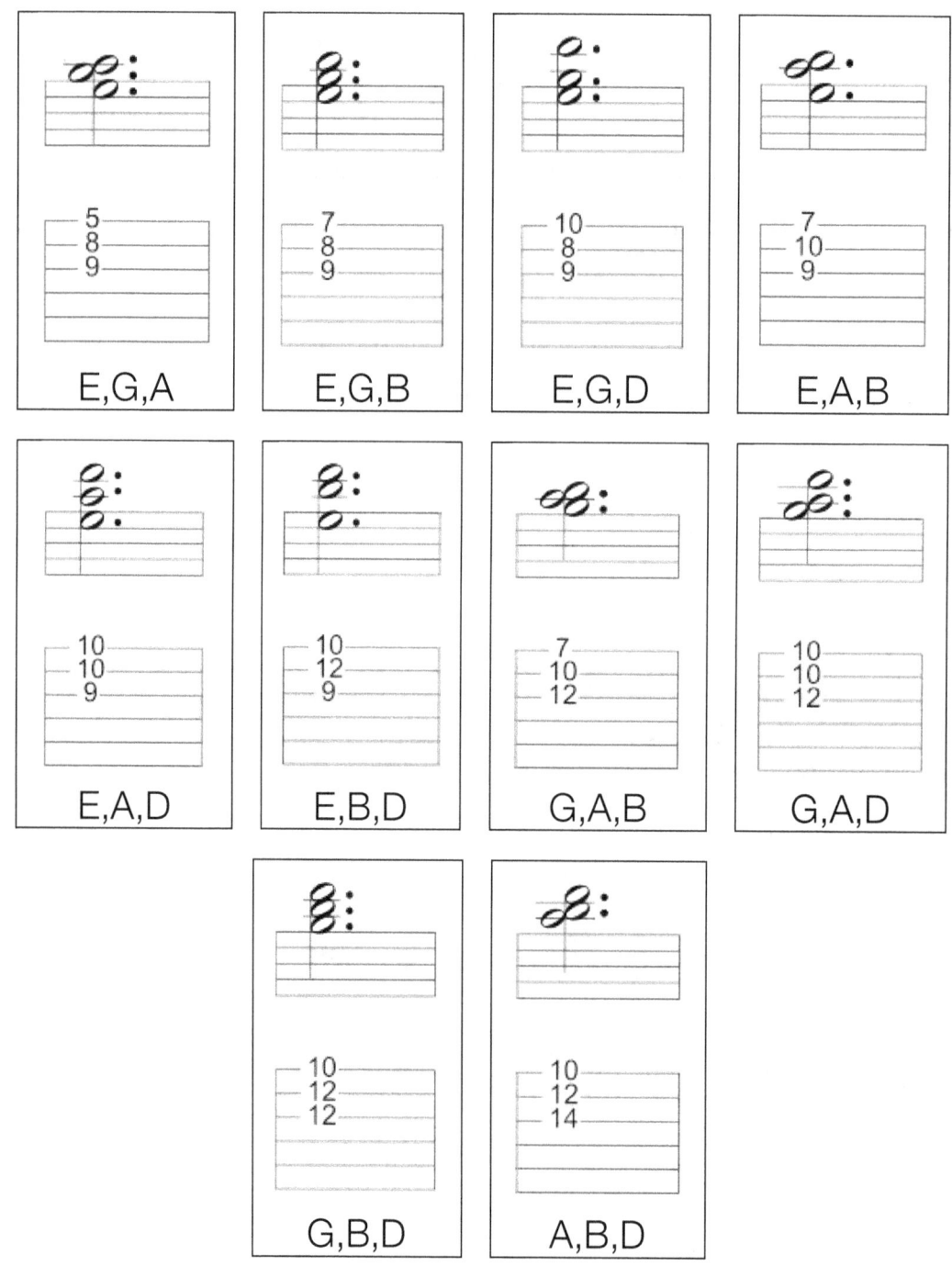

Inversions

Any triad has six possible inversions. For example, the three-note voicing EGA could be played as:

E-G-A	E-A-G	G-A-E	G-E-A	A-E-G	A-G-E

For analytical purposes, triadic inversions should probably be viewed as one chord as there is a negligible harmonic difference between E-G-A and E-A-G. <u>Sonically</u>, however, the voicings used in any chord are a completely different story.

While any initial voicing could have been used, I've presented the three notes as displaced octaves using the E, D and high E string in the example below. While they all have a similar tonal quality, the overall effect of each one is quite different.

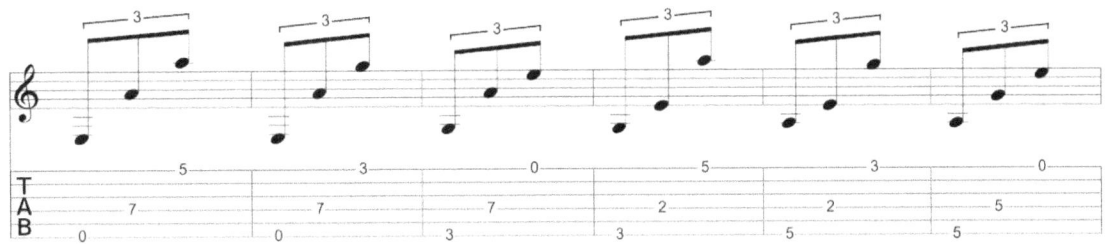

E-G-A	E-A-G	G-A-E	G-E-A	A-E-G	A-G-E

I'll talk more about these inversions and applications more in the *tetrachord* (four-note) section.

"Poor Man's Counterpoint"
(or applying voice leading to comping chords)

Here's something I think is a cool harmonic application of minor pentatonic triad voicings.

I tend to look at broad harmonic structures rather than getting hung up on learning a million individual chord voicings. One trick I use along these lines when comping on a vamp is a method I call "poor man's counterpoint".

In this approach, I take an initial chord voicing and then use *oblique motion* (where one voice changes while the others stay the same) and/or contrary motion to gradually change chords (and generate some interesting musical ideas while doing so).

In this example:

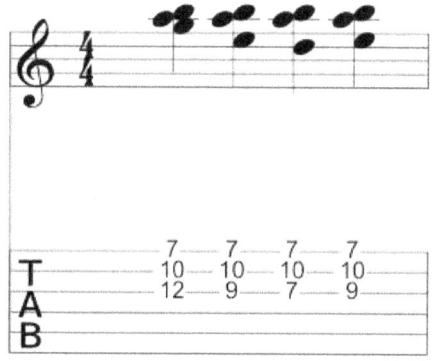

I've taken a cluster voicing and moved one voice on the G string to create a little melodic motion. In a song, the bass and harmony I'd play this against would play a huge role in my specific approach as I'm not thinking of specific theoretical voicings here. I'm thinking about moving notes in the scale and using my ears (and my eyes) to guide which notes I'm moving to.

I've taken this oblique motion idea a little further below and added some contrary motion (one voice goes up while one goes down) on the last chord. I've added the open G as a type of droning pitch as well, but it could have just as easily been any open string on the guitar. As always, experiment and find sounds that work for you!!

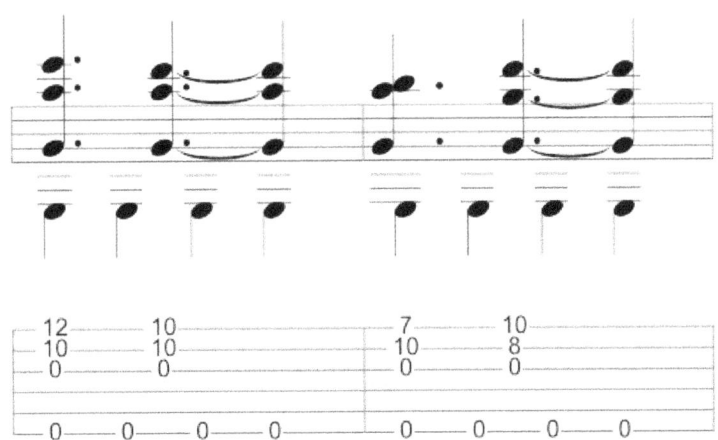

In the final example, I've taken a three bar excerpt of voicings I'd use to create motion over an E minor chord. Notice that the notes on the B string only change twice.

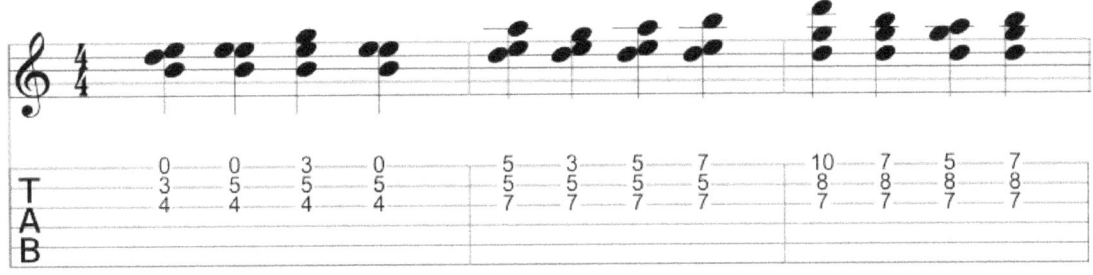

In addition to sounding cool, this approach is a great technical exercise as well in that keeping the notes ringing while you change individual voices can be really challenging! Strive to keep the notes ringing and long as possible!

Pentatonic Harmony: Tetrachords

There are five unique four-note chords (aka tetrachords) in any pentatonic scale based on scale degree.

| 1,2,3,4 | 1,2,3,5 | 1,2,4,5 | 1,3,4,5 | 2,3,4,5 |

Continuing our use of E Minor Pentatonic, the following unique tetrachords are derived (I've used a close voicing but any voicing could be utilized).

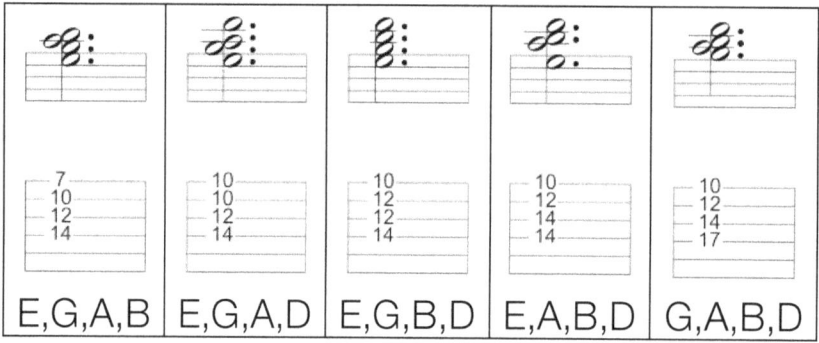

| E,G,A,B | E,G,A,D | E,G,B,D | E,A,B,D | G,A,B,D |

Each tetrachord has twenty four possible inversions based on chord degree:

1-2-3-4	2-3-1-4	3-4-1-2	4-1-2-3
1-2-4-3	2-3-1-4	3-4-2-1	4-1-3-2
1-3-2-4	2-4-1-3	3-1-2-4	4-2-1-3
1-3-4-2	2-4-3-1	3-1-4-2	4-2-1-3
1-4-2-3	2-1-3-4	3-2-1-4	4-3-1-2
1-4-3-2	2-1-4-3	3-2-4-1	4-3-2-1

68

The following examples demostrate some sample arpegiations of the E, G, A, B variations. Using a similar approach to the three-note voicings, I've spread these out over multiple strings to create diferent textures but this process can (and should) be applied to multiple voicings.

Here are the E, G, A, B variations starting from the first note, E.

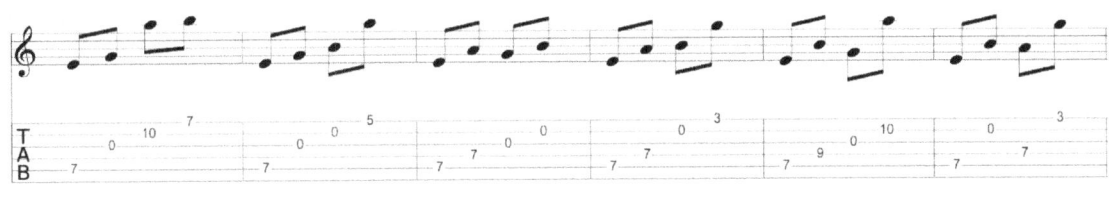

| 1-2-3-4 | 1-2-4-3 | 1-3-2-4 | 1-3-4-2 | 1-4-2-3 | 1-4-3-2 |

Here are the E, G, A, B variations starting from the second note, G.

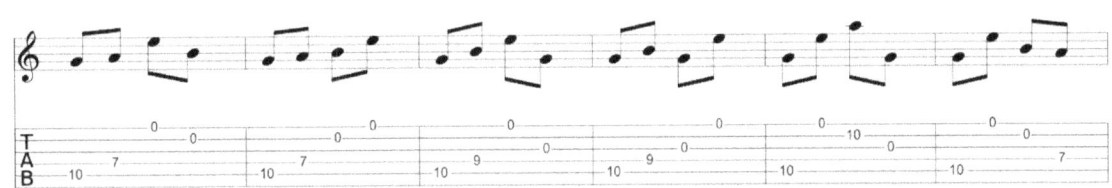

| 2-3-1-4 | 2-3-4-1 | 2-4-1-3 | 2-4-3-1 | 2-1-3-4 | 2-1-4-3 |

Here are the E, G, A, B variations starting from the third note, A.

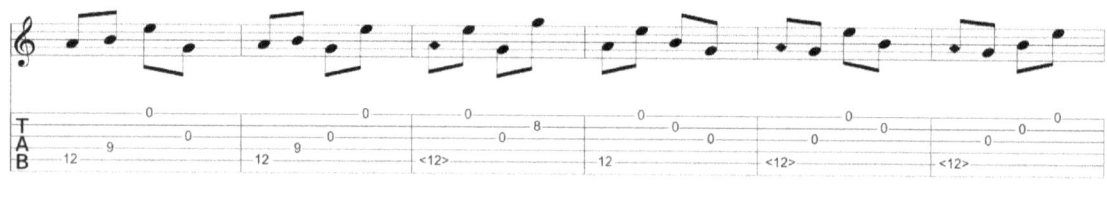

| 3-4-1-2 | 3-4-2-1 | 3-1-2-4 | 3-1-4-2 | 3-2-1-4 | 3-2-4-1 |

Finally, here are the E, G, A, B variations starting from the fourth note, B.

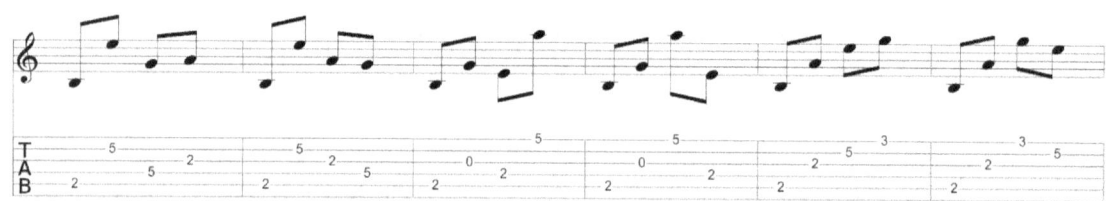

| 4-1-2-3 | 4-1-3-2 | 4-2-1-3 | 4-2-1-3 | 4-3-1-2 | 4-3-2-1 |

Additionally, it's good to remember that in terms of inversions:

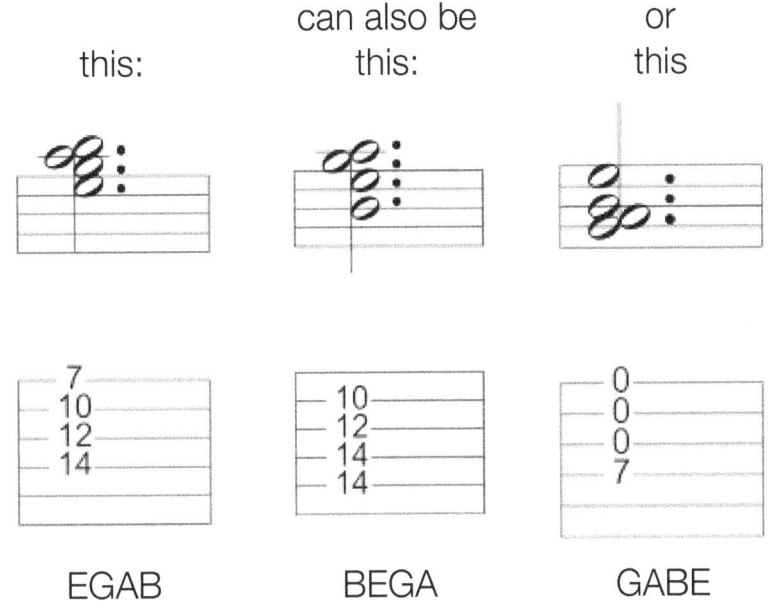

this:	can also be this:	or this
EGAB	BEGA	GABE

Or even this:

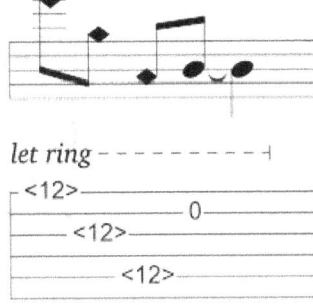

In general, I recommend that you don't be afraid to move things around to positions and voicings that sound cool and work for you!

Section VI:

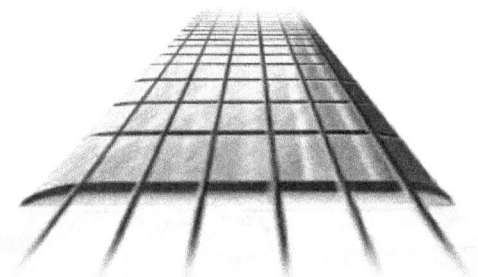

Pentatonic Index

The Pentatonic Scale Index

The following material has been excerpted from my *GuitArchitect's Guide To Chord Scales* book. If you find this material interesting, you might want to check out that book as well.

Reading the Index

What I've done with this index is mark out all possible five-note scales (i.e. pentatonics) using unique notes. I've done this by marking out the chromatic scale on a straight line like so:

R	♭2	2	#2/♭3	3	4	#4/♭5	5	#5/♭6	6/♭♭7	#6/♭7	7

And then writing in the scale formula below it. Writing the scale in this format allows you to "see" the scale on a single string

Here it is in table form:

R	♭2	2	#2/♭3	3	4	#4/♭5	5	#5/♭6	6/♭♭7	#6/♭7	7
Open String	1st Fret	2nd Fret	3rd Fret	4th Fret	5th Fret	6th Fret	7th Fret	8th Fret	9th Fret	10th Fret	11th Fret

For example the scale formula for a minor pentatonic scale is:

Root, ♭3, 4, 5, ♭7

Here it is in table form:

R	♭2	2	#2/♭3	3	4	#4/♭5	5	#5/♭6	6/♭♭7	#6/♭7	7
R			♭3		4		5			♭7	

Here it is in table form and notation:

R	♭2	2	#2/♭3	3	4	#4/♭5	5	#5/♭6	6/♭♭7	#6/♭7	7
R			♭3		4		5			♭7	
TAB 0			TAB 3		TAB 5		TAB 7			TAB 10	

Here it is in notation and tablature.

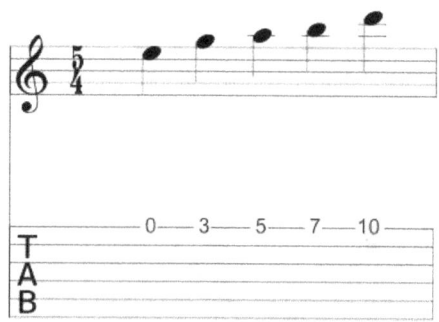

Root (E), ♭3 (G), 4(A), 5(B), ♭7(D)

This type of systematic process could be applied to any scale, but a list of all possible scales with unique notes can be found in *The GuitArchitect's Guide To Chord Scales*.

The "Baker's Dozen" Pentatonic Scale

A baker's dozen is where a 13th item is thrown in for free in an order of any twelve of the same thing at a bakery. This +1 concept can also be applied to pentatonic scales where adding a 6th note creates a "baker's dozen pentatonic".

There are seven variations for possible minor pentatonic + 1 variations.

Minor Pentatonic +1 Scales

R	♭2	2	#2/♭3	3	4	#4/♭5	5	#5/♭6	6/♭♭7	#6/♭7	7
R	♭2		♭3		4		5			♭7	
R		2	♭3		4		5			♭7	
R			♭3	3	4		5			♭7	
R			♭3		4	#4/♭5	5			♭7	
R			♭3		4		5	♭6		♭7	
R			♭3		4		5		6	♭7	
R			♭3		4		5			♭7	7

The most famous example of the Minor Pentatonic + 1 scale is the blues scale which uses a #4/♭5 to create a six note scale. In the following examples, I'll show a few organic approaches I use to get some extra notes into my pentatonic-based ideas.

In a solo, instead of just using E Minor Pentatonic (E, G, A, B and D) an E minor chord, I could also use B Minor Pentatonic (B, D, E, F♯ and A).

Quick tip - when soloing over a minor chord you can substitute a minor chord a 5th away (e.g. playing B Minor Pentatonic over an E minor chord).

Closer inspection reveals that the only difference between the two scales is the F♯ and the G. Since both notes sound good against E minor, using both of them produces a six-note scale (E, F♯, G, A, B and D). Here's a sample fingering of the combined scales in the 12th position.

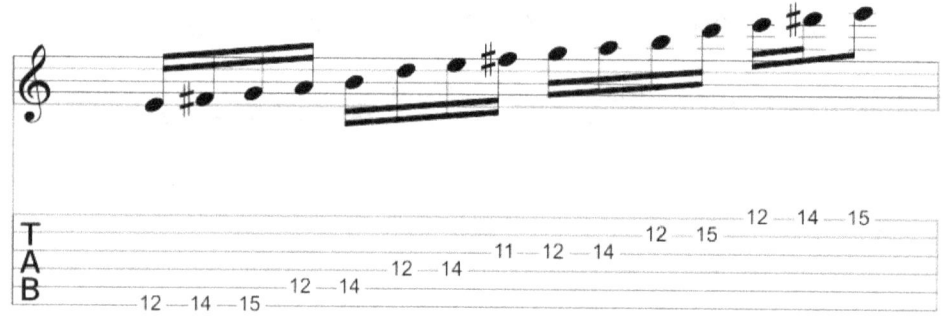

If fingered as a two-string scale, the same fingering pattern can be moved in octaves which eliminates the need for multiple fingerings.

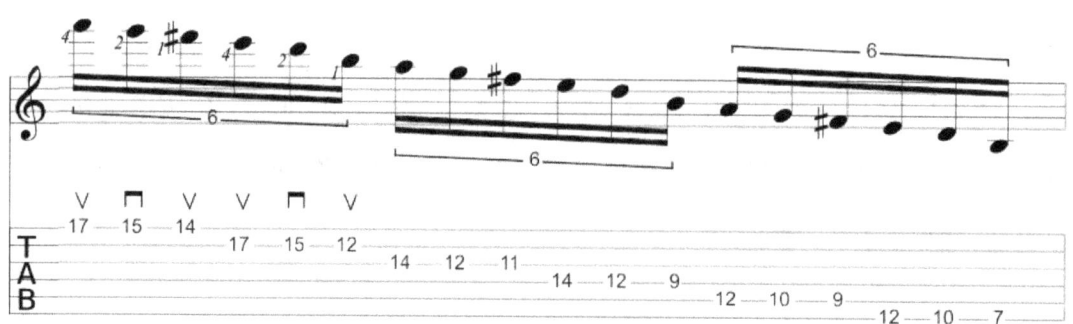

In contrast, here it is ascending:

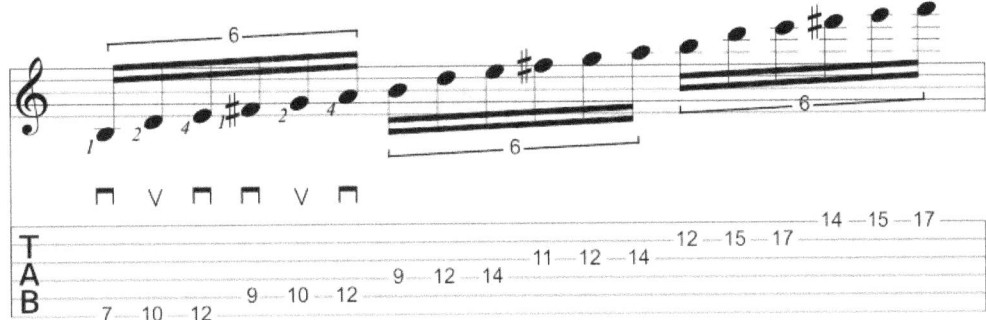

The picking pattern is the same for each string but when I switch strings its two down picks in a row. You can use alternate picking if you're use to that approach as well but I try to apply the same picking pattern to all three-note per string patterns.

Practicing the pattern

In addition to focusing on the timing of the notes, it's very important to practice slowly and only increase speed when both the timing (are all the notes being played with rhythmic equivalence?), tone (i.e. can you hear all of the notes clearly?) and hand tension (is your hand should be as relaxed as possible?) are all working together.

This *is* challenging - particularly if you're not used to the stretch – but practicing properly in small focused increments consistently and increasing steadily over time will yield deep long term results in your playing.

Here's another way to manipulate the patterns into something more fluid. Taking Pattern 3 (from the two-string patterns on page 32) and doubling the D creates a six-note pattern with the same fingering on both strings. This works best as a descending line to my ears:

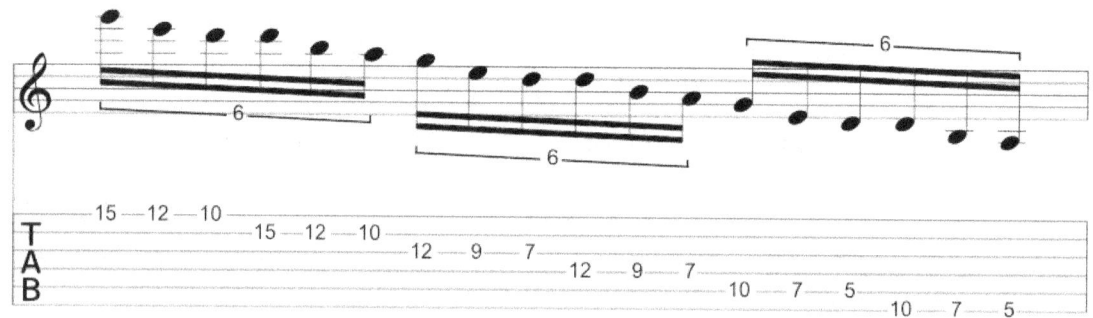

The following uses the same idea with Pattern 4 (also from the two-string patterns on page 33) and has a doubled E.

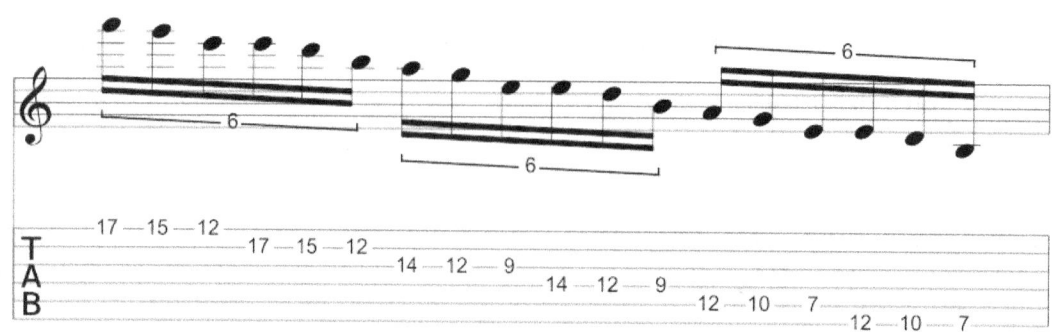

Section VII:

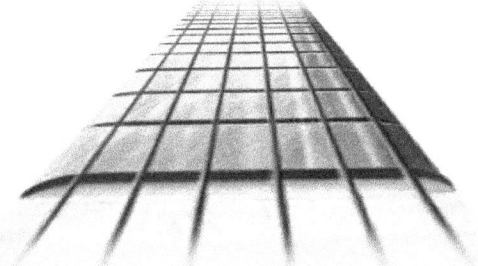

Additional Tips

Using This Book

I'm closing with a recommendation for how to *really* get something from this book, but I also encourage you to approach the material in whatever way works for you.

In improvisation, the goal is to be able to hear what you're going to play before you actually play it.

Singing what you play is probably the best way to internalize it and make it your own. Here are some steps that can help:

- Start with just one pattern or fret board shape and sing the notes as you play it.

- Try playing those notes and then singing them <u>without</u> playing them. If you can't do this, do what George Benson does in his soloing and sing while you play the notes (to work towards the goal of being able to sing without the notes).

- Alter the note order and try alternating between playing and singing phrases – to paraphrase W.A. Matthieu, "play what you sing and sing what you play". Explore variations like alternating between playing one note and singing the next.

- The point of these approaches is to associate a shape with a sound so you can realize/modify that sound in real time.

In general, I don't recommend spending a lot of time practice forms that you're not likely to use. One idea applied well is worth more than a dozen ideas applied poorly.

Finally, if you take melodic and harmonic ideas and incorporate them into what you're doing you're more likely to retain them. Take these ideas, use them in riffs, soloing or comping to make them your own, usurp them and ultimately, please, make some music with them.

Best wishes on your journey.

Section VIII:

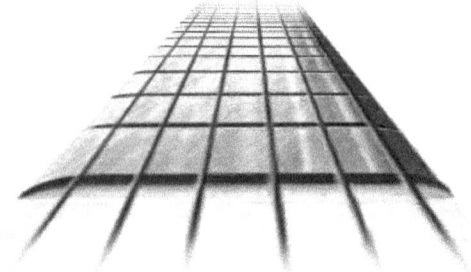

Index

Chord Tones And Interval Review/Overview

Chord tones and *chord formulas* are used as a way of analyzing chord qualities. Chord Tones are derived from intervals in the major scale. In this case, an *interval* refers to the distance between two notes. Intervals and chord tones are often used interchangeably, so having some familiarity with both terms will ultimately be helpful to you.

For example: In the C Major scale, the note D is the 2nd scale degree so the interval from C → D is a Major 2nd. **Intervals are assumed to be major unless otherwise stated.** Exceptions to this rule are found in both the 4th and 5th scale degrees which are referred to as *Perfect Intervals*.

C Major Interval Chart

Initial Pitch	Second Pitch	Interval
C	D	Major 2nd
C	E	Major 3rd
C	F	Perfect 4th
C	G	Perfect 5th
C	A	Major 6th
C	B	Major 7th

Musicians typically refer to sharped scale degrees as either *sharp* (ex. ♯5) or *augmented* (ex. "+5").

Flatted scale degrees, are either referred to as *flat* (ex. ♭3) or *minor* (ex. "minor 3rd or min. 3rd ").

The following chart will show all of the possible intervals from the root within one octave.

Let's look at a C major scale that ascends over two octaves:

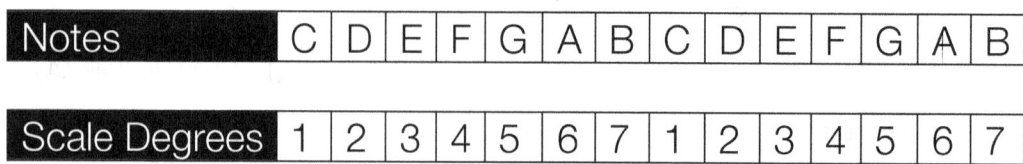

Notes	C	D	E	F	G	A	B	C	D	E	F	G	A	B
Scale Degrees	1	2	3	4	5	6	7	1	2	3	4	5	6	7

Underneath this chart, I'll add another row of scale degrees but this time I'll let those numbers keep ascending:

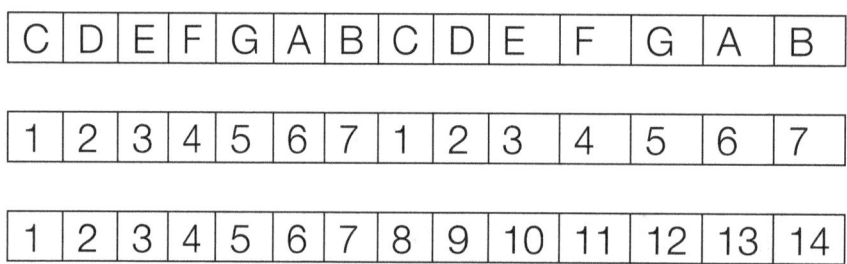

C	D	E	F	G	A	B	C	D	E	F	G	A	B
1	2	3	4	5	6	7	1	2	3	4	5	6	7
1	2	3	4	5	6	7	8	9	10	11	12	13	14

One very common way to build chords in western music involves using every other note of a scale. Now let's use this process with the above diagram, this time eliminating every other note.

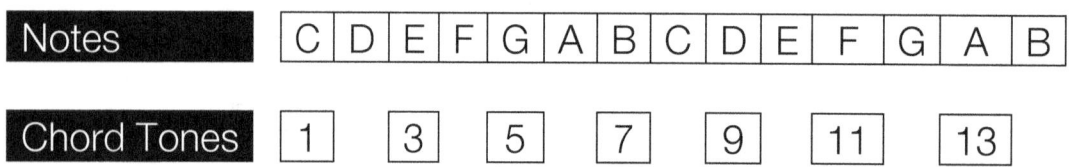

Notes	C	D	E	F	G	A	B	C	D	E	F	G	A	B
Chord Tones	1		3		5		7		9		11		13	

As you can see, when building chords with stacked 3rds after the 7th scale degree, we refer to the additional tones by their upper chord tone name (i.e. 9, 11 or 13) instead of their lower octave name (2, 4 or 6).

Chords and scales are basically the same thing. The difference being that chords are a group of notes played at the same time, producing a harmony and scales are a group of notes played individually.

The following chart will help illustrate the relationship between interval names (and chord tones).

C Major Interval/Chord Tone Chart (Multi-Octave)

Root	Second Pitch	Interval Name	Chord tone
C	D♭	Minor 2nd (or ♭2nd)	Minor 9th (or ♭9th)
C	D	Major 2nd	Major 9th
C	D♯	♯2nd	♯9th
C	E♭	Minor 3rd (or ♭3rd)	Minor 3rd (or ♭3rd)
C	E	Major 3rd	Major 3rd
C	F	Perfect 4th	11th
C	F♯	♯4th	♯11th
C	G♭	♭5th	♭5th
C	G	Perfect 5th	Perfect 5th
C	G♯	♯5th	♯5th
C	A♭	Minor 6th (or ♭6th)	Minor 13th (or ♭13th)
C	A	Major 6th	Major 13th
C	A♯	♯6th	♯13th
C	B♭	Minor 7th (or ♭7th)	Minor 7th (or ♭7th)
C	B	Major 7th	Major 7th

Chord Formula Guide

The following guide is by no means comprehensive, but should serve as a reference for the general qualities of chords you might see on a Real Book tune or a session chart.

In major scale harmony there are 3 basic triadic qualities (major, minor, and diminished), with a 4th triad, the augmented chord, appearing in melodic and harmonic minor.

Since the 3rd is the defining element of overal traidic quality, triads can be further simplified into two groups:

chords with major 3rds (major and augmented) and

chords with minor 3rd (minor and diminished).

(augmented and diminished chords have also been grouped here.)

While there are four basic tetrachordal qualities in major scale harmony (major 7th, minor 7th, dominant 7th and minor7♭5 - aka 1/2 diminished), some varitions that arise from melodic and harmonic minor harmonizations have been included here as well. Using these tones, any chord can be analyzed using variations on the following formulas. I've included some general tips to help decipher chord formulas on each page.

Chord Formula Guide – Major 3rd Based

Major	R, 3, 5
6th	R, 3, 5, 6
7th	R, 3, 5, 7
7th +	R, 3, ♯5, 7
9th	R, 3, 5, 7, 9
9th +	R, 3, ♯5, 7, 9
(add 9 or /9)	R, 3, 5, 9
6/9	R, 3, 5, 6, 9
7/6	R, 3, 5, 6, 7
+11	R, 3, 5, 7, 9, ♯11
13	R, 3, 5, 7, 9, 13
Augmented	R, 3, ♯5
7th	R, 3, ♯5, 7

Chord Shortcuts:

Any major chord always has a major 3rd.

Any major 7th chord always has a major 3rd and a major 7th.

Any augmented chord always has a major 3rd and a sharp 5th.

The 11th is generally considered an "avoid" tone on major chords.

Any other chord modifications will be listed in the formula. (ex. "maj7♯5")

Chord Formula Guide - Minor 3rd Based

Triad	R, ♭3, 5
6	R, ♭3, 5, 6
7th	R, ♭3, 5, ♭7
7♭5	R, ♭3, ♭5, ♭7
Maj. 7th	R, ♭3, 5, 7
9th	R, ♭3, 5, ♭7, 9
(add 9) or /9	R, ♭3, 5, 9
6/9	R, ♭3, 5, 6, 9
Maj. 9 or m7/9	R, ♭3, 5, 7, 9
11	R, ♭3, 5, ♭7, 11
13	R, ♭3, 5, ♭7, 9, 13
Diminished	R, ♭3, ♭5
7th	R, ♭3, ♭5, ♭♭7

Chord Shortcuts:

Any minor chord always has a minor 3rd.

Any minor 7th chord always has a minor 3rd and a minor 7th.

Any diminished chord always has a minor 3rd and a flat 5th.

Any other chord modifications will be listed in the formula. (ex. "min7♭5").

Chord Formula Guide – Dominant 7th Based

7th	R, 3, 5, ♭7
7/6	R, 3, 5, 6, ♭7
7/11	R, 3, 5, ♭7, 11*
7sus	R, 4, 5, ♭7
7/6 sus	R, 4, 5, 6, ♭7
9th	R, 3, 5, ♭7, 9
11th	R, 3, 5, ♭7, 9, 11*
7+11	R, 3, 5, ♭7, 9, ♯11
13th	R, 3, 5, ♭7, 9, 13
13sus	R, 4, 5, ♭7, 9, 13
7/6/11	R, 3, 5, 6, ♭7, 11*, 13
11/13	R, 3, 5, ♭7, 9, 11*, 13

Chord Shortcuts:

7th, 9th, 11th and 13th chords are dominant *unless* it specifically says major or minor (example Major 7th or Minor 7th).

Some players consider the 11th to be an avoid tone on dominant 7th chords.

Any other chord modifications will be listed in the formula. (ex. "7♯5").

(See the Altered Dominant section for more examples).

Chord Formula Guide – Altered Dominant

7♭5	R, 3, ♭5, ♭7
7♯5	R, 3, ♯5, ♭7
7♭9	R, 3, 5, ♭7, ♭9
7♯9	R, 3, 5, ♭7, ♯9
7♭9♭5	R, 3, ♭5, ♭7, ♭9
7♭9♯5	R, 3, ♯5, ♭7, ♭9
7♯9♯5	R, 3, ♯5, ♭7, ♯9
7♯9♭5	R, 3, ♭5, ♭7, ♯9
9 +	R, 3, ♯5, ♭7, 9
9♭5	R, 3, ♭5, ♭7, 9
9♯5♭5	R, 3, ♭5, ♯5, ♭7, 9
11♭9	R, 3, 5, ♭7, ♭9, 11
+ 11	R, 3, 5, ♭7, 9, ♯11
13♭9	R, 3, 5, ♭7, ♭9, 13
13♯9	R, 3, 5, ♭7, ♯9, 13
13+11	R, 3, 5, ♭7, 9, ♯11,13

90

Pentatonic Tonal Center Chart

Tonal Center		E MInor Pentatonic			
	E	G	A	B	D
E	R	♭3	11	5	♭7
F	7	9	3	♯11	13
F♯ / G♭	♭7	♭9	♭3/ ♯9	11	♭13/ ♯5
G	13	R	9	3	5
G♯ / A♭	♭13	7	♭9	♭3/ ♯9	♭5/♯11
A	5	♭7	R	9	11
A♯ / B♭	♭5/♯11	13	7	♭9	3
B	11	♭13	♭7	R	♭3
C	3	5	13	7	9
C♯ /D♭	♭3/ ♯9	♭5/♯11	♭13	♭7	♭9
D	9	11	5	13	R
D♯ /E♭	♭9	3	♭5/♯11	♭13	7

91

Note-Per-String Patterns For All Six Strings

1-1-1-1-1-1	1-1-1-1-1-2	1-1-1-1-1-3
1-1-1-1-2-1	1-1-1-1-2-2	1-1-1-1-2-3
1-1-1-1-3-1	1-1-1-1-3-2	1-1-1-1-3-3

1-1-1-2-1-1	1-1-1-2-1-2	1-1-1-2-1-3
1-1-1-2-2-1	1-1-1-2-2-2	1-1-1-2-2-3
1-1-1-2-3-1	1-1-1-2-3-2	1-1-1-2-3-3

1-1-1-3-1-1	1-1-1-3-1-2	1-1-1-3-1-3
1-1-1-3-2-1	1-1-1-3-2-2	1-1-1-3-2-3
1-1-1-3-3-1	1-1-1-3-3-2	1-1-1-3-3-3

1-1-2-1-1-1	1-1-2-1-1-2	1-1-2-1-1-3
1-1-2-1-2-1	1-1-2-1-2-2	1-1-2-1-2-3
1-1-2-1-3-1	1-1-2-1-3-2	1-1-2-1-3-3

1-1-2-2-1-1	1-1-2-2-1-2	1-1-2-2-1-3
1-1-2-2-2-1	1-1-2-2-2-2	1-1-2-2-2-3
1-1-2-2-3-1	1-1-2-2-3-2	1-1-2-2-3-3

1-1-2-3-1-1	1-1-2-3-1-2	1-1-2-3-1-3
1-1-2-3-2-1	1-1-2-3-2-2	1-1-2-3-2-3
1-1-2-3-3-1	1-1-2-3-3-2	1-1-2-3-3-3

1-1-3-1-1-1	1-1-3-1-1-2	1-1-3-1-1-3
1-1-3-1-2-1	1-1-3-1-2-2	1-1-3-1-2-3
1-1-3-1-3-1	1-1-3-1-3-2	1-1-3-1-3-3

1-1-3-2-1-1	1-1-3-2-1-2	1-1-3-2-1-3
1-1-3-2-2-1	1-1-3-2-2-2	1-1-3-2-2-3
1-1-3-2-3-1	1-1-3-2-3-2	1-1-3-2-3-3

1-1-3-3-1-1	1-1-3-3-1-2	1-1-3-3-1-3
1-1-3-3-2-1	1-1-3-3-2-2	1-1-3-3-2-3
1-1-3-3-3-1	1-1-3-3-3-2	1-1-3-3-3-3

Note-Per-String Patterns For All Six Strings

1-2-1-1-1-1	1-2-1-1-1-2	1-2-1-1-1-3
1-2-1-1-2-1	1-2-1-1-2-2	1-2-1-1-2-3
1-2-1-1-3-1	1-2-1-1-3-2	1-2-1-1-3-3

1-2-1-2-1-1	1-2-1-2-1-2	1-2-1-2-1-3
1-2-1-2-2-1	1-2-1-2-2-2	1-2-1-2-2-3
1-2-1-2-3-1	1-2-1-2-3-2	1-2-1-2-3-3

1-2-1-3-1-1	1-2-1-3-1-2	1-2-1-3-1-3
1-2-1-3-2-1	1-2-1-3-2-2	1-2-1-3-2-3
1-2-1-3-3-1	1-2-1-3-3-2	1-2-1-3-3-3

1-2-2-1-1-1	1-2-2-1-1-2	1-2-2-1-1-3
1-2-2-1-2-1	1-2-2-1-2-2	1-2-2-1-2-3
1-2-2-1-3-1	1-2-2-1-3-2	1-2-2-1-3-3

1-2-2-2-1-1	1-2-2-2-1-2	1-2-2-2-1-3
1-2-2-2-2-1	1-2-2-2-2-2	1-2-2-2-2-3
1-2-2-2-3-1	1-2-2-2-3-2	1-2-2-2-3-3

1-2-2-3-1-1	1-2-2-3-1-2	1-2-2-3-1-3
1-2-2-3-2-1	1-2-2-3-2-2	1-2-2-3-2-3
1-2-2-3-3-1	1-2-2-3-3-2	1-2-2-3-3-3

1-2-3-1-1-1	1-2-3-1-1-2	1-2-3-1-1-3
1-2-3-1-2-1	1-2-3-1-2-2	1-2-3-1-2-3
1-2-3-1-3-1	1-2-3-1-3-2	1-2-3-1-3-3

1-2-3-2-1-1	1-2-3-2-1-2	1-2-3-2-1-3
1-2-3-2-2-1	1-2-3-2-2-2	1-2-3-2-2-3
1-2-3-2-3-1	1-2-3-2-3-2	1-2-3-2-3-3

1-2-3-3-1-1	1-2-3-3-1-2	1-2-3-3-1-3
1-2-3-3-2-1	1-2-3-3-2-2	1-2-3-3-2-3
1-2-3-3-3-1	1-2-3-3-3-2	1-2-3-3-3-3

Note-Per-String Patterns For All Six Strings

1-3-1-1-1-1	1-3-1-1-1-2	1-3-1-1-1-3
1-3-1-1-2-1	1-3-1-1-2-2	1-3-1-1-2-3
1-3-1-1-3-1	1-3-1-1-3-2	1-3-1-1-3-3

1-3-1-2-1-1	1-3-1-2-1-2	1-3-1-2-1-3
1-3-1-2-2-1	1-3-1-2-2-2	1-3-1-2-2-3
1-3-1-2-3-1	1-3-1-2-3-2	1-3-1-2-3-3

1-3-1-3-1-1	1-3-1-3-1-2	1-3-1-3-1-3
1-3-1-3-2-1	1-3-1-3-2-2	1-3-1-3-2-3
1-3-1-3-3-1	1-3-1-3-3-2	1-3-1-3-3-3

1-3-2-1-1-1	1-3-2-1-1-2	1-3-2-1-1-3
1-3-2-1-2-1	1-3-2-1-2-2	1-3-2-1-2-3
1-3-2-1-3-1	1-3-2-1-3-2	1-3-2-1-3-3

1-3-2-2-1-1	1-3-2-2-1-2	1-3-2-2-1-3
1-3-2-2-2-1	1-3-2-2-2-2	1-3-2-2-2-3
1-3-2-2-3-1	1-3-2-2-3-2	1-3-2-2-3-3

1-3-2-3-1-1	1-3-2-3-1-2	1-3-2-3-1-3
1-3-2-3-2-1	1-3-2-3-2-2	1-3-2-3-2-3
1-3-2-3-3-1	1-3-2-3-3-2	1-3-2-3-3-3

1-3-3-1-1-1	1-3-3-1-1-2	1-3-3-1-1-3
1-3-3-1-2-1	1-3-3-1-2-2	1-3-3-1-2-3
1-3-3-1-3-1	1-3-3-1-3-2	1-3-3-1-3-3

1-3-3-2-1-1	1-3-3-2-1-2	1-3-3-2-1-3
1-3-3-2-2-1	1-3-3-2-2-2	1-3-3-2-2-3
1-3-3-2-3-1	1-3-3-2-3-2	1-3-3-2-3-3

1-3-3-3-1-1	1-3-3-3-1-2	1-3-3-3-1-3
1-3-3-3-2-1	1-3-3-3-2-2	1-3-3-3-2-3
1-3-3-3-3-1	1-3-3-3-3-2	1-3-3-3-3-3

94

Note-Per-String Patterns For All Six Strings

2-1-1-1-1-1	2-1-1-1-1-2	2-1-1-1-1-3
2-1-1-1-2-1	2-1-1-1-2-2	2-1-1-1-2-3
2-1-1-1-3-1	2-1-1-1-3-2	2-1-1-1-3-3

2-1-1-2-1-1	2-1-1-2-1-2	2-1-1-2-1-3
2-1-1-2-2-1	2-1-1-2-2-2	2-1-1-2-2-3
2-1-1-2-3-1	2-1-1-2-3-2	2-1-1-2-3-3

2-1-1-3-1-1	2-1-1-3-1-2	2-1-1-3-1-3
2-1-1-3-2-1	2-1-1-3-2-2	2-1-1-3-2-3
2-1-1-3-3-1	2-1-1-3-3-2	2-1-1-3-3-3

2-1-2-1-1-1	2-1-2-1-1-2	2-1-2-1-1-3
2-1-2-1-2-1	2-1-2-1-2-2	2-1-2-1-2-3
2-1-2-1-3-1	2-1-2-1-3-2	2-1-2-1-3-3

2-1-2-2-1-1	2-1-2-2-1-2	2-1-2-2-1-3
2-1-2-2-2-1	2-1-2-2-2-2	2-1-2-2-2-3
2-1-2-2-3-1	2-1-2-2-3-2	2-1-2-2-3-3

2-1-2-3-1-1	2-1-2-3-1-2	2-1-2-3-1-3
2-1-2-3-2-1	2-1-2-3-2-2	2-1-2-3-2-3
2-1-2-3-3-1	2-1-2-3-3-2	2-1-2-3-3-3

2-1-3-1-1-1	2-1-3-1-1-2	2-1-3-1-1-3
2-1-3-1-2-1	2-1-3-1-2-2	2-1-3-1-2-3
2-1-3-1-3-1	2-1-3-1-3-2	2-1-3-1-3-3

2-1-3-2-1-1	2-1-3-2-1-2	2-1-3-2-1-3
2-1-3-2-2-1	2-1-3-2-2-2	2-1-3-2-2-3
2-1-3-2-3-1	2-1-3-2-3-2	2-1-3-2-3-3

2-1-3-3-1-1	2-1-3-3-1-2	2-1-3-3-1-3
2-1-3-3-2-1	2-1-3-3-2-2	2-1-3-3-2-3
2-1-3-3-3-1	2-1-3-3-3-2	2-1-3-3-3-3

Note-Per-String Patterns For All Six Strings

2-2-1-1-1-1	2-2-1-1-1-2	2-2-1-1-1-3
2-2-1-1-2-1	2-2-1-1-2-2	2-2-1-1-2-3
2-2-1-1-3-1	2-2-1-1-3-2	2-2-1-1-3-3

2-2-1-2-1-1	2-2-1-2-1-2	2-2-1-2-1-3
2-2-1-2-2-1	2-2-1-2-2-2	2-2-1-2-2-3
2-2-1-2-3-1	2-2-1-2-3-2	2-2-1-2-3-3

2-2-1-3-1-1	2-2-1-3-1-2	2-2-1-3-1-3
2-2-1-3-2-1	2-2-1-3-2-2	2-2-1-3-2-3
2-2-1-3-3-1	2-2-1-3-3-2	2-2-1-3-3-3

2-2-2-1-1-1	2-2-2-1-1-2	2-2-2-1-1-3
2-2-2-1-2-1	2-2-2-1-2-2	2-2-2-1-2-3
2-2-2-1-3-1	2-2-2-1-3-2	2-2-2-1-3-3

2-2-2-2-1-1	2-2-2-2-1-2	2-2-2-2-1-3
2-2-2-2-2-1	2-2-2-2-2-2	2-2-2-2-2-3
2-2-2-2-3-1	2-2-2-2-3-2	2-2-2-2-3-3

2-2-2-3-1-1	2-2-2-3-1-2	2-2-2-3-1-3
2-2-2-3-2-1	2-2-2-3-2-2	2-2-2-3-2-3
2-2-2-3-3-1	2-2-2-3-3-2	2-2-2-3-3-3

2-2-3-1-1-1	2-2-3-1-1-2	2-2-3-1-1-3
2-2-3-1-2-1	2-2-3-1-2-2	2-2-3-1-2-3
2-2-3-1-3-1	2-2-3-1-3-2	2-2-3-1-3-3

2-2-3-2-1-1	2-2-3-2-1-2	2-2-3-2-1-3
2-2-3-2-2-1	2-2-3-2-2-2	2-2-3-2-2-3
2-2-3-2-3-1	2-2-3-2-3-2	2-2-3-2-3-3

2-2-3-3-1-1	2-2-3-3-1-2	2-2-3-3-1-3
2-2-3-3-2-1	2-2-3-3-2-2	2-2-3-3-2-3
2-2-3-3-3-1	2-2-3-3-3-2	2-2-3-3-3-3

Note-Per-String Patterns For All Six Strings

2-3-1-1-1-1	2-3-1-1-1-2	2-3-1-1-1-3
2-3-1-1-2-1	2-3-1-1-2-2	2-3-1-1-2-3
2-3-1-1-3-1	2-3-1-1-3-2	2-3-1-1-3-3

2-3-1-2-1-1	2-3-1-2-1-2	2-3-1-2-1-3
2-3-1-2-2-1	2-3-1-2-2-2	2-3-1-2-2-3
2-3-1-2-3-1	2-3-1-2-3-2	2-3-1-2-3-3

2-3-1-3-1-1	2-3-1-3-1-2	2-3-1-3-1-3
2-3-1-3-2-1	2-3-1-3-2-2	2-3-1-3-2-3
2-3-1-3-3-1	2-3-1-3-3-2	2-3-1-3-3-3

2-3-2-1-1-1	2-3-2-1-1-2	2-3-2-1-1-3
2-3-2-1-2-1	2-3-2-1-2-2	2-3-2-1-2-3
2-3-2-1-3-1	2-3-2-1-3-2	2-3-2-1-3-3

2-3-2-2-1-1	2-3-2-2-1-2	2-3-2-2-1-3
2-3-2-2-2-1	2-3-2-2-2-2	2-3-2-2-2-3
2-3-2-2-3-1	2-3-2-2-3-2	2-3-2-2-3-3

2-3-2-3-1-1	2-3-2-3-1-2	2-3-2-3-1-3
2-3-2-3-2-1	2-3-2-3-2-2	2-3-2-3-2-3
2-3-2-3-3-1	2-3-2-3-3-2	2-3-2-3-3-3

2-3-3-1-1-1	2-3-3-1-1-2	2-3-3-1-1-3
2-3-3-1-2-1	2-3-3-1-2-2	2-3-3-1-2-3
2-3-3-1-3-1	2-3-3-1-3-2	2-3-3-1-3-3

2-3-3-2-1-1	2-3-3-2-1-2	2-3-3-2-1-3
2-3-3-2-2-1	2-3-3-2-2-2	2-3-3-2-2-3
2-3-3-2-3-1	2-3-3-2-3-2	2-3-3-2-3-3

2-3-3-3-1-1	2-3-3-3-1-2	2-3-3-3-1-3
2-3-3-3-2-1	2-3-3-3-2-2	2-3-3-3-2-3
2-3-3-3-3-1	2-3-3-3-3-2	2-3-3-3-3-3

Note-Per-String Patterns For All Six Strings

3-1-1-1-1-1	3-1-1-1-1-2	3-1-1-1-1-3
3-1-1-1-2-1	3-1-1-1-2-2	3-1-1-1-2-3
3-1-1-1-3-1	3-1-1-1-3-2	3-1-1-1-3-3

3-1-1-2-1-1	3-1-1-2-1-2	3-1-1-2-1-3
3-1-1-2-2-1	3-1-1-2-2-2	3-1-1-2-2-3
3-1-1-2-3-1	3-1-1-2-3-2	3-1-1-2-3-3

3-1-1-3-1-1	3-1-1-3-1-2	3-1-1-3-1-3
3-1-1-3-2-1	3-1-1-3-2-2	3-1-1-3-2-3
3-1-1-3-3-1	3-1-1-3-3-2	3-1-1-3-3-3

3-1-2-1-1-1	3-1-2-1-1-2	3-1-2-1-1-3
3-1-2-1-2-1	3-1-2-1-2-2	3-1-2-1-2-3
3-1-2-1-3-1	3-1-2-1-3-2	3-1-2-1-3-3

3-1-2-2-1-1	3-1-2-2-1-2	3-1-2-2-1-3
3-1-2-2-2-1	3-1-2-2-2-2	3-1-2-2-2-3
3-1-2-2-3-1	3-1-2-2-3-2	3-1-2-2-3-3

3-1-2-3-1-1	3-1-2-3-1-2	3-1-2-3-1-3
3-1-2-3-2-1	3-1-2-3-2-2	3-1-2-3-2-3
3-1-2-3-3-1	3-1-2-3-3-2	3-1-2-3-3-3

3-1-3-1-1-1	3-1-3-1-1-2	3-1-3-1-1-3
3-1-3-1-2-1	3-1-3-1-2-2	3-1-3-1-2-3
3-1-3-1-3-1	3-1-3-1-3-2	3-1-3-1-3-3

3-1-3-2-1-1	3-1-3-2-1-2	3-1-3-2-1-3
3-1-3-2-2-1	3-1-3-2-2-2	3-1-3-2-2-3
3-1-3-2-3-1	3-1-3-2-3-2	3-1-3-2-3-3

3-1-3-3-1-1	3-1-3-3-1-2	3-1-3-3-1-3
3-1-3-3-2-1	3-1-3-3-2-2	3-1-3-3-2-3
3-1-3-3-3-1	3-1-3-3-3-2	3-1-3-3-3-3

Note-Per-String Patterns For All Six Strings

3-2-1-1-1-1	3-2-1-1-1-2	3-2-1-1-1-3
3-2-1-1-2-1	3-2-1-1-2-2	3-2-1-1-2-3
3-2-1-1-3-1	3-2-1-1-3-2	3-2-1-1-3-3

3-2-1-2-1-1	3-2-1-2-1-2	3-2-1-2-1-3
3-2-1-2-2-1	3-2-1-2-2-2	3-2-1-2-2-3
3-2-1-2-3-1	3-2-1-2-3-2	3-2-1-2-3-3

3-2-1-3-1-1	3-2-1-3-1-2	3-2-1-3-1-3
3-2-1-3-2-1	3-2-1-3-2-2	3-2-1-3-2-3
3-2-1-3-3-1	3-2-1-3-3-2	3-2-1-3-3-3

3-2-2-1-1-1	3-2-2-1-1-2	3-2-2-1-1-3
3-2-2-1-2-1	3-2-2-1-2-2	3-2-2-1-2-3
3-2-2-1-3-1	3-2-2-1-3-2	3-2-2-1-3-3

3-2-2-2-1-1	3-2-2-2-1-2	3-2-2-2-1-3
3-2-2-2-2-1	3-2-2-2-2-2	3-2-2-2-2-3
3-2-2-2-3-1	3-2-2-2-3-2	3-2-2-2-3-3

3-2-2-3-1-1	3-2-2-3-1-2	3-2-2-3-1-3
3-2-2-3-2-1	3-2-2-3-2-2	3-2-2-3-2-3
3-2-2-3-3-1	3-2-2-3-3-2	3-2-2-3-3-3

3-2-3-1-1-1	3-2-3-1-1-2	3-2-3-1-1-3
3-2-3-1-2-1	3-2-3-1-2-2	3-2-3-1-2-3
3-2-3-1-3-1	3-2-3-1-3-2	3-2-3-1-3-3

3-2-3-2-1-1	3-2-3-2-1-2	3-2-3-2-1-3
3-2-3-2-2-1	3-2-3-2-2-2	3-2-3-2-2-3
3-2-3-2-3-1	3-2-3-2-3-2	3-2-3-2-3-3

3-2-3-3-1-1	3-2-3-3-1-2	3-2-3-3-1-3
3-2-3-3-2-1	3-2-3-3-2-2	3-2-3-3-2-3
3-2-3-3-3-1	3-2-3-3-3-2	3-2-3-3-3-3

Note-Per-String Patterns For All Six Strings

3-3-1-1-1-1	3-3-1-1-1-2	3-3-1-1-1-3
3-3-1-1-2-1	3-3-1-1-2-2	3-3-1-1-2-3
3-3-1-1-3-1	3-3-1-1-3-2	3-3-1-1-3-3

3-3-1-2-1-1	3-3-1-2-1-2	3-3-1-2-1-3
3-3-1-2-2-1	3-3-1-2-2-2	3-3-1-2-2-3
3-3-1-2-3-1	3-3-1-2-3-2	3-3-1-2-3-3

3-3-1-3-1-1	3-3-1-3-1-2	3-3-1-3-1-3
3-3-1-3-2-1	3-3-1-3-2-2	3-3-1-3-2-3
3-3-1-3-3-1	3-3-1-3-3-2	3-3-1-3-3-3

3-3-2-1-1-1	3-3-2-1-1-2	3-3-2-1-1-3
3-3-2-1-2-1	3-3-2-1-2-2	3-3-2-1-2-3
3-3-2-1-3-1	3-3-2-1-3-2	3-3-2-1-3-3

3-3-2-2-1-1	3-3-2-2-1-2	3-3-2-2-1-3
3-3-2-2-2-1	3-3-2-2-2-2	3-3-2-2-2-3
3-3-2-2-3-1	3-3-2-2-3-2	3-3-2-2-3-3

3-3-2-3-1-1	3-3-2-3-1-2	3-3-2-3-1-3
3-3-2-3-2-1	3-3-2-3-2-2	3-3-2-3-2-3
3-3-2-3-3-1	3-3-2-3-3-2	3-3-2-3-3-3

3-3-3-1-1-1	3-3-3-1-1-2	3-3-3-1-1-3
3-3-3-1-2-1	3-3-3-1-2-2	3-3-3-1-2-3
3-3-3-1-3-1	3-3-3-1-3-2	3-3-3-1-3-3

3-3-3-2-1-1	3-3-3-2-1-2	3-3-3-2-1-3
3-3-3-2-2-1	3-3-3-2-2-2	3-3-3-2-2-3
3-3-3-2-3-1	3-3-3-2-3-2	3-3-3-2-3-3

3-3-3-3-1-1	3-3-3-3-1-2	3-3-3-3-1-3
3-3-3-3-2-1	3-3-3-3-2-2	3-3-3-3-2-3
3-3-3-3-3-1	3-3-3-3-3-2	3-3-3-3-3-3

Possible Note Orders For Any Pentatonic Scale

12345	23451	34512	45123	51234
12354	23415	34521	45132	51243
12435	23514	34125	45231	51342
12453	23541	34152	45213	51324
12534	23145	34215	45312	51423
12543	23154	34251	45321	51432
13245	24135	35124	41235	52341
13254	24153	35142	41253	52314
13452	24351	35241	41352	52413
13425	24315	35214	41325	52431
13524	24513	35412	41523	52434
13542	24531	35421	41532	52143
14235	25134	31245	42351	53412
14253	25143	31254	42315	53421
14352	25341	31452	42513	53124
14325	25314	31425	42531	53142
14523	25413	31524	42135	53241
14532	25431	31542	42153	53214
15234	21345	32451	43512	54123
15243	21354	32415	43521	54132
15342	21453	32514	43125	54231
15324	21435	32541	43152	54213
15423	21534	32145	43251	54312
15432	21543	32154	43215	54321

Minor Pentatonic +1 Scales

R	♭2	2	#2/♭3	3	4	#4/♭5	5	#5/♭6	6/♭♭7	#6/♭7	7
R	♭2		♭3		4		5			♭7	
R		2	♭3		4		5			♭7	
R			♭3	3	4		5			♭7	
R			♭3		4	#4/♭5	5			♭7	
R			♭3		4		5	♭6		♭7	
R			♭3		4		5		6	♭7	
R			♭3		4		5			♭7	7

Other Books In *The GuitArchitect's Guide To* Series

I have several other reference / instructional books available for purchase. If you're looking for new ways to explore the fretboard, or looking for new sounds to investigate, these books are for you!!!

The GuitArchitect's Guide to Modes: Melodic Patterns

The original book! At 333 pages this is the deepest guide to melodic variations out there! Thousands of ideas await you on every page.

The GuitArchitect's Positional Exploration

The GuitArchitect's Positional Exploration shows how to take a simple idea and modify it through melodic, harmonic and rhythmic variations that you can apply to your own music.

The GuitArchitect's Guide To Modes: Harmonic Combinatorics

In GuitArchitect's Guide to Modes: Harmonic Combinatorics, I explain how to construct and analyze chords and create thousands of variations and progressions from a single chord using a unique visualization method. *Harmonic Combinatorics* is a vast harmonic and melodic resource for guitarists. With this approach, you can create an almost infinite number of unique melodic phrases and harmonic devices to compose or improvise your own music.

The GuitArchitect's Guide To Chord Scales

In an easy, intuitive and musical way, I explain how to make your own scales to play over chords and how to derive chords from whatever scales you create. *The GuitArchitect's Guide To Chord Scales* is an extensive instruction method and a reference book that explains chord scale options ranging from 3-notes to the full 12-note chromatic scale. While primarily an instructional, compositional and improvisational resource for guitarists, *Chord Scales* is a vital addition to any musician's library.

The GuitArchitect's Guide To Symmetrical Twelve-Tone Patterns

In *The GuitArchitect's Guide To Symmetrical Twelve-Tone Patterns*, I've taken the approaches from his previous books *Melodic Patterns* and *Guide To Chord Scales* and applied them to a rigorous examination of twelve-tone patterns that can be used as melodic, harmonic, improvisational or compositional resources. Eschewing academic jargon, *Symmetrical Twelve-Tone Patterns* is an intuitive and accessible methodology that will help guitarists develop new sounds.

Print editions of any of the books are available individually from Amazon or Lulu.com. Full information for book ordering can be found at guitarchitecture.org.

The Book Bundle

I've created a digital bundle of files to accompany the material in this book. The bundle contains:

- Two Guitar Pro files (one in GP6 format and one in GP5). Guitar Pro is a musical notation and tablature platform that I've used to create all of the notated examples in this book. Guitar Pro also works well as a phrase trainer, which could be of tremendous benefit to the reader of this text as both a way to hear the examples without a guitar as well as a means to practice getting the examples up to speed. The Guitar Pro file contains all of the musical examples in the text. Readers without Guitar Pro may also want to check out free alternatives for playback such as TuxGuitar or Web Tab Player.

- A MIDI file (exported from the same material).

- MP3s of the MIDI musical examples (again, exported from the same material).

This bundle is free to anyone who has purchased the book. Simply send me an e-mail at guitar.blueprint@gmail.com and I'll send it to you.

Please Note: While a free trial version of Guitar Pro can be downloaded from the Guitar Pro website (http://www.guitar-pro.com), you'll need the full version of the software to open the .gpx files.